About the author

CHRISTINE HARVEY has been hailed as 'the guru of profit and personal motivation', and is an award-winning sales executive in her own right. After starting three successful companies of her own, she now travels the world teaching top-flight executives how to sell, how to manage, and how to motivate.

YOUR PURSUIT OF PROFIT, which Christine Harvey co-authored, was a bestseller in six languages. Her seminars pack the house repeatedly in London, the USA, Singapore, Brussels and Stockholm, and she holds the unique privilege of being the first woman to have been featured in TOKYO BUSINESS TODAY.

Christine Harvey is American-born and resident in London. She runs her own sales training company and is Chairman of the London Chamber of Commerce West Section. She is also on the board of several enterprise agencies and companies.

CHRISTINE HARVEY

Secrets of the World's Top Sales Performers

BOB ADAMS, INC.
PUBLISHERS
Holbrook, Massachusetts

First published in Great Britan by
Business Books Limited
An imprint of Century Hutchinson Limited/London

United States edition published by
Bob Adams, Inc.
260 Center Street
Holbrook, MA 02343

ISBN 1-55850-852-X

Contents

CONTENTS

CONTENTS

Preface:
How this book was
written and why

I can't remember a six-month period of my life that has been as continually stimulating as this.

Before leaving London last week, I sent a card to Frances Kelly, my agent, which had a phrase printed inside saying 'Thank you for brightening up my day'. I crossed out 'day' and put 'year' in its place.

'Thanks for helping me make this book happen,' I told her. 'This has been a most fascinating and rewarding experience.'

To talk to ten top achievers of the world, to exchange ideas and philosophies, to hear their life stories, and to probe for what really makes them tick, has kept me constantly motivated.

I first had the idea for a study like this 12 years ago when I was in sales and marketing management in the computer industry.

I walked into the MD's office in London where I was based and said, 'Dave, I've got a great idea. We have some real high flyers in this company selling in different parts of the world.

'I want to find out how one woman in Miami can earn three times the commission everyone else is earning, every year. What makes her consistently do it?'

I suggested to him that we get the support of the company president and carry out a study. 'We'll follow the high flyers for two days. We'll find out their strategies. We'll document exactly what they say. We'll find out how they do their planning, etc., etc.'

I reasoned from my own experience in selling that this would give everyone in sales a short cut to success. Why not learn from the best and stop trying to reinvent the wheel in our own microcosm?

The MD liked the idea, but his fears held him back. 'What will the president think? After all, we have people whose job it is to train salespeople. Maybe he'll think we're not doing our job right.'

The idea has played on my mind ever since. Wouldn't it be useful to prove the universal truths about excellent salesmanship which others could follow?

Wouldn't it be interesting to see how these same principles are applied by people in all industries to get the best results?

Following the success of *Your Pursuit of Profit* in England, which went into seven foreign editions within two years of release (Dutch, French, German, Swedish, American, Australia and Japanese), my agent had been 'gently' persuading me to do another book. (When you work with Frances, the word 'gentle' takes on a new perspective.)

'I do have one great idea. But, Frances, I'm up to my eyes in seminars,' I told her as I explained the idea. 'I'm going to Australia for one seminar next month and then to Singapore for another. When I'm back, I've got speaking engagements. And my husband and I have promised ourselves more vacation time.'

'Never mind,' she said, 'the idea is great. You can do the interviews as you travel, between your seminars. You know how you are, you can't stand a dull moment anyway. You'll love it.'

The next thing I knew, she was on the phone again saying Century Hutchinson loved the idea too. They thought it had tremendous worldwide appeal.

When could I start, she asked. That was eight months ago and it seems like yesterday. The people I've met are the most positive and inspiring you'd hope to meet. Their principles are high. Their ethics are high. Their hopes for mankind are high. Their enthusiasm is contagious.

As I wrote the final chapter I reflected on what I, myself, had gained.

I thought about what Michael Renz kept saying to me during the Mercedes interview: 'To teach is to learn.' He was referring to his own experience in training other people to sell.

I thought about myself and my role as the 'interpreter' between what my high flyers said and how I put it across to you.

I had to absorb it, to rehash it and then to teach it. And each time I learned.

I thought about what Micheline Notteboom said in Chapter 4 about the finesses of things. It's really the fine points that make the difference.

The more you delve, the more you see. The more profound the principles become.

It's been a wonderfully rewarding experience to see the principles, which Bill Sykes and I profess in our first book and in our seminars, come alive in so many ways, in so many countries, in so many industries.

It's been wonderful to create a new circle of friends around the world and to share in their lives. I had a call at midnight last week from Australia. It was Bob Broadley: 'What time is it there? I've been trying to get you all week,' he said. 'I've read the chapter, it's great.'

'Thanks, Bob,' I said. 'How are Maree and the kids?' 'Maree's up north getting some sun. Everything's great,' he said with the enthusiasm that only an Australian can put across.

'Aren't Australians terrific,' I said to my husband Tom, as I hung up, still half asleep. 'That must have been Bob Broadley,' he said. It made me think about how much the book and its people had become so much a part of both our lives – in fact the lives of everyone we know.

My hope is that it will become a significant part of your life, too. I hope that the people and their personalities will come alive for you – that their techniques will jump out at you, either in the chapters or the action sections, and that you'll be able to adapt them to your life to achieve the positive results you're looking for.

As I'm putting the final touches to the manuscript and getting ready to board the plane – this time for Australia to run a motivation seminar – I'm thinking over Frances Kelly's words. She's right. I can't stand a dull moment and I *did* love it.

Christine Harvey
19 November 1988

Foreword

by Bill Sykes

I was thrilled to receive one of Christine Harvey's transatlantic telephone calls recently and be asked to write this foreword. In recent years, Christine and I have spent many hours in meetings and telephone calls on both sides of the Atlantic, planning and working together on many different projects.

The variety of projects has included co-authoring our first book, *Your Pursuit of Profit*, and developing sales and marketing training programmes for senior executives which are now taught at management institutes around the world. And, through our consulting practices, helping foreign companies to establish themselves in new overseas markets. In each of these endeavours, we would not have succeeded had it not been for Christine's vision and unbridled enthusiasm to make things happen – excellently – while pursuing her numerous other ventures of consulting, motivational speaking and TV appearances.

This new book by Christine Harvey is unique. Through her own pursuit of excellence and dedication to succeed, Christine has travelled the world to search out the special stories from the very best in the field of selling. These are important people. They have related to Christine their thoughts and insights, and they have given their reasons for their phenomenal successes.

Christine has highlighted the common traits and special techniques which set these people apart and make them not just 'good' salespeople, but the best. We can all apply these principles of success in our daily lives, whether or not we are professional salespeople. After all, we are all called upon to sell something at some time. We sell ideas, new products, new programmes, old cars, and a myriad different items throughout our lives.

Christine Harvey has given us the opportunity to learn from the best in the world. For that we thank Christine, and the only story which is missing and, I know, modesty prevents her from relating, is Christine's own.

Bill Sykes is the British co-author of 'Your Pursuit of Profit': 1986, 2nd ed. 1988

CHAPTER ONE

The Competitive Edge

"You can do anything anyone else can do"

JONATHAN WEAL

London and Chicago

Financial Futures Capital Markets International/Geldermanns

"I'll never forget the comment my maths teacher wrote on my end of year report – lost."

Yet there he was a few years later, in one of the most competitive, financially oriented industries in the world . . . and, at the TOP.

You could argue that a success pattern is established in early childhood. Not so. Jonathan Weal came last in his class at school. He challenged the educational system. If he wasn't interested in a subject, he took it with a grain of salt. But it didn't destroy his confidence. There were too many interesting things in life to get bogged down with the uninteresting.

RECOGNIZE AND MOTIVATE HIGH ACHIEVERS

It's amazing how often in life the great achievers were told in childhood that they were hopeless.

The message is loud and clear. When trying to motivate ourselves or others, we need to look below the surface. The academic grade card told us nothing about Jonathan's potential.

At age ten he had a team of four people washing cars. At 13 he was reading the *Financial Times*. At 14 he was skipping school to buy and sell antiques, and at 22 he was the youngest to reach an executive position in a major bank.

Jonathan Weal has a ten-year reputation in London for building a customer base from nothing. At 29, among the fiercest competition of financial futures trading, he's brought himself up from starting point to the top – not once but three times, in three different companies.

At 19, with no academic qualifications, he took his first step into trading, with County Bank, part of the National Westminster Group. Since then he has lead three teams of people to the top. First with Conti Commodities, then with Cargill, and finally with his own company,

Capital Markets International, trading under the umbrella of Geldermanns.

One company Jonathan worked for was threatened with closure and he was suddenly left overseeing and motivating a team of five people. His income in that first struggling year with them was £45,000, then it shot up to £110,000, then £150,000, then £190,000 and, finally in the fifth year, £230,000. Most of us would be happy with a five-year increase of that magnitude!

Due to his efforts, the office threatened with closure stayed open. By the second year it was the most profitable in the company. Imagine – going from the threat of closure to the most profitable position in two years.

Now with his own company, Jonathan believes wholeheartedly in four precepts:

- Don't sell something you don't believe in.
- Know your subject and build mutual respect with your customers.
- Always have an active prospects list which you contact regularly.
- Learn from the questions people ask you.

With his four-step process, Jonathan has managed to bring his company to the top of the list against his two highest competitors. He did this in only one year while the competitors had been in business for five years.

But, long before that, Jonathan made a name for himself in the industry by building a trust relationship. 'I don't recommend something to a customer unless I believe in it,' he says. 'I ask myself, "If I was in the same position as the bank which is my client, would I do it?" If the answer is "yes", I recommend it. If not, I use the "forget it" policy.

'Clients know you're not infallible. When I'm wrong, I'm willing to castigate myself. *Other competitors try to hide bad recommendations and that's where they go wrong.* People only trust you when they know the up and down side.'

DON'T PATRONIZE THE CLIENT

'I'm always straight with my clients. I don't believe they respect you when you try to make them think they're your best friend or you act subservient.'

On the day we visited Jonathan, lunch was a squash game with a client. 'Who won?' I asked. 'I beat him,' was the reply, 'I don't believe in patronizing my clients.'

HAVE AN ACTIVE PROSPECT LIST, WITH SYSTEMS OF ATTACK

On prospecting, Jonathan says, 'Always, but always, have a list of people you are in contact with but haven't converted into a sale.

'These might be people who aren't ready for the product or who are dealing with someone else. Keep in touch with them on a regular basis. We speak to some prospects weekly and some bi-monthly. We pass on information that can be of use to them.

'When the times comes, they'll remember you. Also, if they think you have something of use to them, they feel uncomfortable taking something for nothing for too long. As such, your time will come.'

Jonathan likes to keep his systems simple and workable. Every morning a list of clients and prospects is circulated on a clipboard to all the brokers. Everyone checks off the clients they've called and the list is periodically looked at to make sure everyone is called according to the predetermined frequency – daily, weekly, bi-monthly, monthly.

In talking with Jonathan I reflected on my own experience with companies. A lot of business is lost because people follow up a lead only once or twice and then it goes in to what I've jokingly called 'lead heaven'. In other words, it gets absorbed into a file box never to be resurrected. Or it falls to the bottom of the brief case, the floor of the car, or the jacket pocket!

Jonathan's philosophy is that every prospect can be won eventually: 'I don't mind how long it takes me.' He knows that by presenting different strategies to prospects he will eventually find an angle which appeals to them.

EDUCATE THE CLIENT

By directing the customer's interest to a related area, he often gets the business. 'If we first talk about financial futures, for example, and I see that it is going to be hard to get their business because they are entrenched with another broker, I might go off to a related area that I think might interest them. I spend time educating them in the new area.'

Eventually, it's no surprise, they buy into the related area and come back to buy financial futures as well.

You have to respect Jonathan's persistence. His efforts eventually pay off *double*! He has two products sold instead of one.

I'm often asked in my sales seminars how long you should keep a prospect on your list? A week, a month, a year? Jonathan is happy to have them on the list for two years and more! Persistence counts again and again.

He doesn't waste time in finding prospects either. In a four-day trip to Scandinavia he cold-called 24 prospect banks in four countries.

How many do you think he converted? Twenty-five per cent became clients! And two years later he is still communicating with the other 75 per cent through his daily information telex. These he calls his 'reserve'. He knows there are sales ready to implement as time permits.

He also invests time in people who won't bring immediate results. He calls this the 'mutual benefit' system. These people include those in

Tokyo or New York with whom he would reciprocate information which ultimately helps his customers. It is an extra investment of time, but one that pays high dividends because it helps you bring information to the clients.

'Don't be afraid to tell people you don't know,' he advises. 'They'll find out anyway. Go out and ask people whose knowledge you respect. Then go back to the client with the information.'

To novices and seasoned salespeople alike, his advice is emphatic: 'Always learn from the questions people ask you.' It's better to find out if you don't know. 'If I'm caught once, I never let it happen again.' Good advice for anyone in any field who wants to reach the top.

CREATE A COMPETITIVE EDGE
RESPOND FAST

Creating a competitive edge is something Jonathan has become expert at. Ten years into the business he still flies out of his chair when a customer calls. 'Responding to a customer order *fast*, is the first ingredient of success,' he says.

When we visited Jonathan in his fourth floor office in Mincing Lane in London, we got a line demonstration of what he means by *fast*.

As the light panel flashed, indicating a client call, his entire body went into motion. Every muscle threw him towards the phone and kept him rigid while he shouted price execution orders down the line to his colleagues on the trading floor while the customer listened in.

I thought instantly about all the organizations I've ever worked with. I thought how prosperous they could all be if they were rigidly fixed on *fast* customer service from order, through production, through delivery. I thought of how many more customers could be won and kept in every industry, not just financial futures.

PUT MONEY BEHIND IT

But the *fast* service philosophy doesn't stop there for Jonathan. He knows it's not enough to 'do', you have to let the customer 'know' what you're doing for them. And he is prepared to put his money where his mouth is.

To let customers know exactly what's happened, he's installed a special phone system which allows his customers to hear their order being executed in Chicago instantly, while still on the line in London with him.

The customer is in the know, stress levels are down and there is no need for call backs to clarify what happened.

How much does this special service cost? Well, it's about five times the normal phone equipment cost. But Jonathan believes in investing in order to serve clients' needs.

SUPPLY THE EXTRAS

Shouldn't we all throw our weight behind what we know the customer wants? Think of the results! Jonathan believes, 'Customers need to learn that they can trust you, and you do that by giving the fastest, top quality service every time. When they trust you on one service, you can introduce another, and that means more business.'

But he also believes that you must be consistent: *if you fail once, you're out the door.*

The point is that Jonathan goes out of his way to identify the real needs of his customers and supply the little extras that make a difference. All too often in sales consulting we see people hiding behind the false wall of excuses. 'The price is too high, we can't sell.' Or, 'We have no advantage to offer.'

Jonathan has created the advantage. If the customer want fast price execution, he gives it. When they want information, he gives it. When they want ideas and strategies, he gives them.

KEEP YOUR NAME IN FRONT OF THE CUSTOMER

How do you keep your name in the forefront of people's minds? Many companies in all industries produce newsletters, updates and so on which they use to great advantage. Yet Jonathan's method, again devised to build up trust, purs his reputation on the line, while communicating daily with every client and prospect.

Every morning he writes and distribuies a telex, or fax, in which he makes recommendations on key trades for his clients. He keeps the recommendation there until a profit or loss position is exercised. Day in and day out they build a relationship with Jonathan Weal.

BE INNOVATIVE

Clients need information, ideas and strategies. Jonathan creates his own edge over competition by being more innovative for his clients.

How innovative is more innovative? He uses his quiet time to think of strategies. Every other day at least, he and his team generate a new strategy based on market conditions. They put these ideas to the appropriate clients and find that 85 per cent of the time this brings them the business from one client or another. It's all part of *creating* a competitive edge.

LIFESTYLE

All his clients know he's conscious of physical fitness. 'Let's get together soon for a low alcohol drink,' he says as he winds up a telephone call, explaining that he's on a 1,700 calorie regime, three work-outs a week, and no alcohol for ten weeks.

Having broken both feet in rugby, (the love of his life), he's turned to work-outs. Typically, he arrives at the office at 7 a.m. He immediately prepares his now famous daily telex after watching the news screens and brainstorming with one or two clients. Then twice a week he's off for a work-out at 8.30, and finishes the day between 6 and 8 p.m.

Considering the working lunch squash game, that's a 12-hour day, no matter how you slice it.

But physical fitness is important in order to keep in shape. 'The better you feel physically, the better you feel "upstairs"' says Jonathan. This takes diligence and hard work. For an extra boost, he runs in the London Marathon.

MANAGING HIGH FLYERS WITH SUPPORT

What about managing high flyers? Since they are few and far between we have little experience in managing them.

In one job he had, Jonathan discovered that the company planned to close the London office if the team didn't put it in a profit position in three months. This was only two weeks after he'd started. What would you expect from a high flyer in this situation?

Some of his colleagues wanted to spend long hours in meetings discussing strategy. Jonathan wasn't happy to wait around for marketing department strategy or leads. He knew it was time for action.

He went straight to cold calling. Don't forget, all of his prospects were already using other brokers. He had to sell himself in an overbroked market. Then, using the philosophy of 'don't recommend it, if you don't believe it', he started to get referrals without asking.

With this determination, it doesn't take long to prove oneself. After five weeks his company put him in charge of the office operation and they stayed open!

I asked Jonathan what was important to him in getting management support to reach his goals. 'The most frustration I've felt was from management teams in which only ten per cent were doers. The other 90 per cent were people who either said "no", or "I'll think about it", or they'd delegate the decision. It usually never resurfaces or it gets completely lost in the legal department.'

You can imagine the frustration of a mover and shaker like Jonathan, a man who helped a division go from near closure to the most profitable in two years, to have to face 90 per cent of managers who impede decisions, consciously or not.

Movers and shakers want support and they want it *now*. They identify what bottlenecks there are in the organization and they want them eliminated. They can't do their job without this. They won't settle for mediocrity. When they discover your team won't support them, and never will, they'll move on, or create their own organization.

Life's not easy with high flyers. They often reveal problems (and solutions) about the organization for which you'd pay thousands to a consulting firm to tell you. Yet pride often prevents people from hearing it!

PHILOSOPHY

'Even if I lost it all, I'd start again. When you start out, it's all darn hard work, but you push yourself because you know you want something more than average.'

ETHICS

Ethics are an important part of the job. 'There are certain firms whose business style, in my opinion, borders on the unethical.' He wouldn't consider hiring anyone who had worked for that kind of firm more than six months because to do so would indicate approval of their activities. Jonathan says he likes to work with nice people. 'It's all a game so you might as well enjoy yourself.'

He thrives on building his client base bigger and bigger but without losing the fun of it. What's fun? Well, working successfully with people who everyone gets along with. 'I like to build a reliable team around me. I don't have to ask, "What are you up to?" Some are rock steady, some are spontaneous. We all know each other's strengths and weaknesses.'

BE FAIR

' "Be fair" is another axiom. If a piece of business comes in and someone else has spent more time on it, I pass it on to them.' This creates an atmosphere of loyalty among colleagues. And it comes back to you financially. To go from £45,000 to £230,000 in five years as a commissioned trader means you need the support of your colleagues. You need to work together like a finely-tuned instrument.

ORGANIZATION

Take heart, if you think you must be ultra-organized to be a high flyer. Not so. Other qualities like persistence and determination are more important. Jonathan, for example, thinks of himself as 'not the world's most organized person'. I suspect he's too hard on himself. In watching him work, it's obvious that he knows where everything is.

Nevertheless, on our visit, my research assistant did notice a drawer about three inches deep crammed with papers, which he frequently opened. 'What do you keep in that drawer?' she asked. 'That's what I mean,' he answered, 'I'm not very organized. These are my important papers. I let them accumulate here until I can't open the drawer anymore.'

'How long does that take,' I asked. 'About three days', came the answer. 'Could be worse,' I said, as I thought of my own *three-tier* tray, *each* tray three inches deep waiting for me. 'Sometimes we're just too hard on ourselves.'

ACTION SHEET

Use this sheet, and the action section which follows, to enhance your own sales techniques and achievements.

Ideas for development:
1. *Recognize and motivate high achievers*
2. *Have an active prospect list, with systems of attack*
3. *Create a competitive edge*
4. *Keep your name in front of the customer*
5. *Manage high flyers with support*
Others as they relate to you are — (complete sheet according to your needs)

- Of the above ideas, which one is likely to yield the best results for you?

- What percentage of sales (or performance) increase could realistically be expected?

- How long would it take:
  to develop the idea?
  to get results?

- Who would have to be involved?

- What date should you start?

- What is the first step you should take?

ACTION SECTION

1 Recognize and motivate high achievers

As I talked with Jonathan, I thought about what a good lesson it is for us as managers, and in fact as parents, to look for an angle which interests people when they're learning.

I understand that the Japanese are devoting the decade to raising the intelligence level of the next generation. Imagine! Tackling the intelligence level of a whole generation of people.

In our society we don't even take the time and effort to look for ways to inspire the achievement of one individual. In Jonathan's case people just said he was 'lost' rather than looking for an angle which would capture his interest.

If people show weakness in a certain area, it doesn't mean they're hopeless. It only means they haven't been inspired. Or perhaps they don't see the application for the knowledge.

At my speaking engagements I often ask people how many teachers they ever had who motivated them in their lifetime. Usually they say 'one or two'. Think of it – in a lifetime of education we have from 30 to 40 teachers and only one or two of them are motivating!

Why? Was it because they couldn't motivate? Probably not. It's more likely that they saw their role as teaching rather than motivating.

The truth is that people learn when they are motivated, but how many people in teaching or in management think of themselves as motivators?

Have you let traditional thinking hold you back? If so, what steps can you take to overcome it?

2 Have an active prospect list, with daily systems of attack

How much more income do you want to create next month?

Whether you succeed or fail will depend on one important factor. Do you have a realistic grip on how many prospects it takes to convert *one* to a customer?

Is it ten? Is it eight? It might differ for each industry you sell to.

It also differs from one salesperson to another. The important thing is the law of averages – *your* averages.

If your goal is to double your income next month, and to do that you need six new clients, then you need to know *your* law of averages on converting prospects to clients.

If you convert one out of ten, then you need to see 60 prospects next month to gain six new clients – 15 per week.

More important is your daily system of attack. With five working days, you need to see three prospects per day. If one cancels on Monday, you need to see four on Tuesday. To make the law of averages succeed, you have to keep to the total number.

Take it one step further. In order to see three prospects a day, how many phone calls or letters do you need to send?

The biggest failure of people starting businesses is not to consider the law of averages. They are unrealistic about the sales workload necessary to stay in business. They think business will 'come'. It doesn't.

If you don't know your law of averages, guess at it. Then monitor your conversion results daily and adjust the workload accordingly. How much more income do you want next month? How does that break down into *daily* activity?

3 Create a competitive edge

As Bill Sykes and I showed in our book, *Your Pursuit of Profit*, to increase business, it's essential to have an airtight system for following up prospects.

Companies hire accountants to track every penny in and every penny out. But no one hires a 'lead-tracker' to track every lead in and every action taken.

Clients and prospects have to be sold to *while their interest is at a peak.*

What kind of system do you have for following up prospects while their interest is peaked? Is it airtight like an accounting system?

Does it help you make sure no prospect is forgotten? What steps can you take to create a more effective system?

4 Keep your name in front of the customer

It's said that the brain forgets 80 per cent of what it hears within two days. Chances are that customers forget about our companies, our products and our services faster than we realize.

If you belong to a club or an organization, you've probably noticed that you attend more regularly if there is a regular newsletter or phone call than if you only get a once-a-year bulletin.

The same is true of customers. They respond better with prompters.

Jonathan was innovative and created a daily way of communicating with each client. That has helped him make his mark in the industry. It took creativity and courage to develop, and still takes time and money to do it. He reaps the rewards.

What innovative ideas can you think of for keeping your name in front of the customer? What would it cost in terms of time and effort? What results could you expect?

5 Manage high flyers with support

One day one of my research assistants said to me, 'Christine, you are one of only two people in the world I've ever met who actually listens to ideas. Most managers I've known start to tell me why my idea won't work before the idea is even out of my mouth. It makes me stop telling them my ideas because I know what their response will be.'

Movers and shakers want you to hear their ideas. They want your support *now*. If they don't get support, they move on.

Jonathan's frustration with management teams was that '90 per cent were people who either said "no", or "I'll think about it" '.

Are you turning away good ideas from people who are in the front line and know what the customers' needs are and how to meet them through changes in practices? What steps can you take to support high flyers through listening, considering and taking decisive action?

CHAPTER TWO

Creating Your Own Future

"I open my eyes to see how success works"

JANET LIM
Singapore
Automobile Dealership Borneo Motors – Toyota

At nine, she was helping her mother clean airports. At 14, while going to school, she was working on a farm and a construction site for $5 a day.

Now at 29, with no degree but with vision, stamina and creativity, she's created an income for herself which is five times that of a college graduate.

LET YOURSELF HAVE A VISION

Early childhood experiences can make or break your future. At nine, Janet Lim Lay Yang was helping her mother clean airports on the midnight shift. 'I saw Americans and Australians carrying their big heavy luggage and I said to myself, "I want to have luggage and travel like that someday."'

That seemed like a fantasy at the time. Her parents were farm labourers and very poor. At 14 she helped her mother tear open concrete bags on a construction site for $5 a day. Today, 15 years later, she's earning Singapore $80,000 a year. That's five times the earnings of the average college graduate. It's also $266 a day, which is quite a shift from $5 in 15 years.

Her sisters, who also followed their mother around, have all risen to highly-paid jobs. One sister is a construction site supervisor. With no previous experience she rose from a $200 a month drawing office clerk to a $2,000 a month site foreman. Her brothers, on the other hand, who were limited only to the farm, are still earning peasant wages.

What makes the difference? Exposure, exposure, exposure. The vision of a different way of life.

Janet's motto is to open her eyes and see how success works, then copy, copy, copy. Doesn't that make sense for all of us? She realized early in life that she had to learn to talk to a higher economic level. First, she studied how they communicated. She found out how they did it and copied it. She used to watch the Europeans come into the airport. She watched their style and their mannerisms. She became comfortable with them. She learned to identify with them.

Today that knowledge is indispensable. Today at Borneo Motors, where she's one of the fastest tracks ever witnessed in the company's 29 years, she sells to Eurasians, Chinese, Malaysians and Japanese. She has to live and breathe their style.

In her first year on the job she only sold three cars a month. Then she went to Australia and saw her Toyota counterparts selling 15 vehicles a month. 'I was surprised and asked myself: "How can I achieve this."' Then she reset her goal.

The next year she rose to six cars per month, then nine. This year she's fluctuating between 15 and 21, with only three and a half years in the business.

Her business is already 60 per cent referral! Not bad for such a short time in the industry.

Making and keeping customers happy is her doctrine. She uses truth, loyalty and flair. She learns from complaints and she responds fast.

TELL THE TRUTH

Price negotiation is an important factor in car buying, especially in Singapore. Janet uses truth. She believes that if customers know the base price, they won't mind her making a bit of commission. If they ask for the best price and bargain hard, she says, 'The cost of the car is $50,000. My commission is $400.

'The customer usually doesn't mind if you get a commission because they expect service for it. But they must know the truth.'

Janet takes the attitude that the customer is smarter than the salespeople. 'If they have the money to buy an expensive car, then they have a good job. They know the truth anyway.' So by telling it like it is, Janet contends that she builds up trust with them.

GET THEIR LOYALTY AND ASK FOR REFERRAL BUSINESS

Janet expects loyalty from both sides. She doesn't aim for selling one car. She aims for a lifetime of loyalty. First, she demonstrates her loyalty to them. Then, she asks for their loyalty back. As to how, she shows it first. There are a lot of ways. She'll cut her commission if absolutely necessary, but she lets them know she expects all their business and many referrals. 'When I deliver the car to you, if you find my service is good, please introduce business to me,' she tells them straight out. 'When you buy a car from me, it's not the end. I hope to sell you cars in the future, sell to your friends and get referrals. I'll sell this car to you cheap, but in return will you please refer business to me?'

Yet she realizes price is *not* always the important issue. People want service. 'I never let myself get tired of service,' she says. '*Whatever* their requests, I try hard to fulfil them.'

One customer she recalls wanted fast delivery for his 13-unit orders.

The time requirement made his request almost impossible. She tapped the manpower resources of her company and managed to meet the schedule. Later he said, 'I was really impressed by Janet because she went out of her way so much to help us when we needed it.'

RESPOND FAST

Fast response is also her motto. She carries her pager with her everywhere in order to return calls quickly. She encourages customers to call her at home after hours.

There is typically a two-week delivery period after the order is placed. Therefore, she often finds herself communicating with her customers a dozen times during that period. They want to know about the radio, accessories, rustproofing, insurance and finance. With her 19 average vehicle sales per month, times 12 calls per client, she has at least 10 conversations a day with clients in progress, on top of her prospecting calls and visits.

She spends three to four hours per day on the phone talking to new and old customers plus an hour and a half on paperwork. That's a ten and a half hour day, 10 a.m. until 8.30 p.m., six days per week.

LEARN FROM COMPLAINTS

Many salespeople hold themselves back from talking with customers after the sale for fear of complaints. Not Janet. 'Don't be frightened about complaints,' she advises. 'It's best for them to make their complaint, and you can still learn about your own company from it and improve yourself.' She finds only two or three customers out of a hundred difficult.

'What's the most difficult thing to deal with in your industry?' I asked her. 'The non-payers,' she replied. In her company in Singapore it's the rep's responsibility to get full payment for the car before delivery. Some people balk at it and want to have the car before it's paid, so they can check that everything is OK. She hits it head on, 'You can call me or my manager anytime day or night if there are any problems. But if you don't want to pay, we can't deliver.'

But loyalty doesn't stop at the sale of the car. She keeps in touch with each customer and knows their family intimately. If anyone becomes ill, she's at the hospital. When their birthday comes, they receive a card, and if they've referred a lot of business, a bottle of XO cognac. She finds out their birthday and special events through general conversation. Then she records it and acts on it. When their road tax is up for renewal, she handles it for them. It all adds up to constant contact.

She also believes in building up her clients' confidence. When their business is low, she asks them to be hardworking and do their very best. When their business is good, she believes they should upgrade themselves by buying a new car and keep the 'upward spiral going'. 'Why not upgrade your car?' she asks. 'You deserve it. You've worked hard for it.' And they do.

She lives by the same philosophy by investing in herself. She drives a new car which she bought herself. She believes in looking smart. This helps the customer to respect you.

FLAIR

What makes the difference between a memorable salesperson and one who serves the customer well, but is forgotten?

It's flair. And it's flair that touches people's emotions. Janet knows that people do not live and breathe on logic alone. It's emotion that sticks. After all is said and done, she hits them with one last unexpected touch.

She delivers the car. They love it. They walk around it. They get in it. They start up the engine. They test all the dashboard buttons. Then they walk around it again and open the trunk to check for the spare tyre.

Voilà! Janet has filled the trunk with fresh flowers. They don't expect it. 'Aaah, beautiful flowers,' they say as the aroma hits them.

'When I deliver, if they find my service is good, they are pleased to introduce me to other buyers,' says Janet. The flowers are something special. She didn't really need to do it. It's a gesture for the person. It touches their emotions. It gives a feeling of well-being and caring.

RELATIONSHIP WITH COLLEAGUES

The caring feeling reaches out to others she works with. Her manager John Leung says she conveys a warm open feeling to everyone. She gives a little extra in everything she does.

'Good morning, Boss' is a message she often writes at the top of a note she leaves on his desk asking for his assistance, such as getting documents sent through. She doesn't have to add that personal touch, but she does. And it gets people's support and co-operation.

How do her fellow reps see her? There are 39 reps at Borneo's various locations and 75 sales and marketing people all together. Some, of course, are jealous of this high flyer vying for the number one spot after only three and a half years. But Janet shrugs it off. She's worked hard for it and she, herself, does not believe in jealousy.

'Jealousy can destroy you,' she emphatically believes. If she ever gets tempted to be jealous of others, she stops herself immediately. 'This is a negative use of time. I prefer to think, "It's wonderful that they can do it." It means that I can watch them and learn to do it too.' This attitude, she says, puts her in a good mood. 'I can't be jealous of anyone when I see an opportunity to learn.' She sees it as a way of learning to control her heart.

Some find her methods unorthodox. They feel the flowers are a bit over the top. They misunderstand that the flowers are the icing on the cake, not the cake itself.

If Janet didn't do all the right things building up to sales, the flowers wouldn't work. The flowers come *after* the sale. It's the consolidation touch. Yet people who wish they were achieving better can always find reasons to dismiss the success of others. It seems to be a human trait to excuse ourselves in our own mind for not trying harder, for not reaching the success level we wish we had.

THE LEAD UP TO THE SALE

By watching how her successful colleagues got their business, Janet learned what type of clients they went for – the Japanese, the corporate clients. She tried to keep close to them to see how they talked and what they said. She discovered that the best salespeople took time to assess the client's personality type and then match their style to his or hers.

Now Janet always watches and waits before choosing her style.

Are they the serious type? If so, she talks all business. Are they the joking type? If so, she jokes. Are they the negotiating type? If so, she negotiates. 'I give a bit, they give a bit.'

'Don't talk too much, you spoil it,' she advises. You must tune into the customer's style first.

She believes in having a courteous smile and chit chat in order to put the customer at ease. She never goes in for the sale until the customer is sold on her first.

Her opening approach is simple. 'We have so many models, which one are you interested in?' She opens the car door to show them. Action is important. 'The small gesture of opening the car door shows you're willing to serve them,' she says.

She finds out a lot at the same time. If she opens the wrong door, they always say: 'Oh not this one.' She catches on to which car they want without probing.

Then she guides them to the car, opens the door and shows them all the features. Everything is good. 'Power steering, 16 valves, twin cam – very powerful engine. Power windows, power steering – very good car.'

USE A POSITIVE APPROACH

I noticed in my conversations with Janet that she's trained herself on positivity. 'Very good car,' she says. 'How many times do you say, "Very good car",' I asked. 'Once or twice. Not too much, but always at least once. Customers always need their opinion reinforced. I always try to see their side in a positive way,' she said.

Even when their trade-in car leaves a lot to be desired, Janet makes a positive remark. If the paint is chipped and the condition is bad, she says, 'Not so bad, pretty good. I'll try to give you the best price.'

Even listening to her repeat the story made me feel good. I remembered the times I've traded in cars and how often salespeople tried to tell me how bad the car was in order to bring the trade-in value down. It sent a chill through me. How much better it was, I thought, to use a positive approach like Janet's to win the customer's confidence and build their ego rather than destroying it.

After the customer is in a positive and relaxed frame of mind, she observes them to see how interested they are. She makes sure she sells them on the product before talking price. She makes sure she understands which benefits they are looking for.

Then, when she's sure they are sold on her and on the product, she invites them in, off the hot car lot and into the air-conditioned office. 'Would you like a cold drink in the air-conditioned office out of the hot sun to see the brochure?' If they are interested, they'll come in. This means her timing was right and she has done her legwork in selling them on the product.

Then they move into a small guest room with a sofa and coffee table. They discuss the car and the price. They always sit down. She doesn't believe in talking price while standing.

'I never make my customers feel obligated,' she says. 'High pressure may work once but it doesn't bring back repeat customers.

'I know if they leave without buying, but they trust me, they'll come back. Or they'll send referral business.' If they are unsure about how Toyota compares to other cars, she asks them to go out and see them. She has no qualms about suggesting they test a Honda, Mazda, Mitsubishi or Nissan, her main competitors in the Singapore market.

'If you rush the customer, you'll frighten them away. I never ask them to buy too fast. Import car prices are high. They need time to think about the benefits.' That doesn't mean she doesn't try to close the sale.

'If you please customers in every way and if you meet their needs, they will buy.'

FOLLOW UP

Her follow-up is very structured. If they leave without buying, saying, 'I must think', she asks for their business card. She then categorizes them into one of two groups: very interested or viewers only. If they are very interested, she calls them the next day. If they are viewers only, she waits for them to call.

Her colleagues often ask how she has this uncanny knack of knowing who is serious. 'Easy,' she says. 'If they want to test drive and take away a brochure, they are just curiosity seekers. If they ask the right questions and ask prices, they are serious. I know right away, after ten years in sales, if a person is genuine. It's the way they communicate, the way they speak.' Janet sold jewellery before selling cars and gained expertise in recognizing buying signals.

'What do you do if you think they're serious, but they won't leave a business card?' I asked. 'Then I staple my card in the catalogue', she said. She still gives them the same friendly service. 'If I've said the right thing, they'll come back.'

PHILOSOPHY

Janet learns by watching. She likes to visualize herself in situations before plunging in. Her biggest challenge was cracking the commercial market.

'I remember how scared I was in the beginning to approach the commercial market. One day my boss told me that if I could train myself up to sell fleet cars to the professional and commercial market, it would be much better for my future.

'In my heart I was scared', she confides. But she overcame her fear by taking a colleague along to show her the ropes. She learned how to answer customers' questions – how to tackle them with straight fast answers. She learned she had to control the customer, not let the customer control her, by anticipating questions and knowing the answers.

STAMINA AND DISCIPLINE

'At first I used to work seven days a week, now I work six. The 50 metres I had to walk 15 times a day over bunchy ground carrying water to the pig farm, while also working at the sugar cane plantation when I was young, made me strong.'

In talking with her manager, it's obvious that her stamina and energy level is an important part of her output.

So she doesn't regret her farming background. Instead, she values it for making her strong. What a healthy philosophy, to value rather than resent our backgrounds.

She also believes that national service, which is compulsory for boys, is good for everyone. At school she was in the NCC, National Cadet Corps, where she learned shooting, fast movement and team work. She also feels it was an advantage in becoming comfortable in a disciplined male environment and in learning to care for oneself to a high standard. Ironing uniforms and shining shoes wasn't fun, but provided excellent self discipline. Now, getting down to paperwork and other mundane tasks which require discipline is like water off a duck's back.

THE THREE MOTIVATORS

When she left her $14,000 a year job in jewellery to tackle car sales which offered a base salary of only $190 per month, she knew she had to have confidence in herself to succeed. She told herself that she needed three motivators:

- To like the industry.
- To have the curiosity to learn.
- To have the desire to make money.

Notice that money was third on her list of motivators. It's interesting that surveys over the years consistently reveal that money is the third or fourth motivator for people.

Why? Well, think about it. In sales, the drive for money alone without the skill, without the commitment to the product, without the commitment to improve, will not yield results. Skill and attitude are all-important.

USE POSITIVITY IN EVERYTHING

Janet doesn't just use positivity with customers. She uses it with her own speech pattern about herself. She never looks at what she hasn't achieved, but rather at what she can achieve.

We all know people who hold themselves back saying they haven't got the necessary education. Janet worked on the farm before and after school, from age six to 14, carrying pails of water across her shoulders on a bamboo stick. By the time she reached school she was always exhausted. As a result she didn't get good marks and left school at 18.

But does she have a complex about not having a degree? Not at all.

Instead of feeling belittled, she's proud of herself. 'I know that if I put my heart into it and I'm willing to learn, I can have it.'

Most college graduates earn $12,000 to $18,000 she told me. 'I earn $80,000 and I taught myself what I needed to know to be successful.'

Her whole psyche is tuned to positivity. During my stay in Singapore I was invited to the seafood restaurant at the Goodwood Hotel, a very well-known eating place. I took Janet along. 'Have you been here before?' she was asked. 'This is my first time,' was her reply.

Notice, she didn't say 'no', the negative. She said, 'This is my first time.' This was positive, implying she would come here again.

Janet doesn't just give lip service to her methods of success, she lives them. Whatever she sees and wants, she works for. And she achieves it!

ACTION SHEET

Use this sheet, and the action section which follows, to enhance your own sales techniques and achievements.

Ideas for development:
1. *Let yourself have a vision*
2. *Tell the truth*
3. *Get customers' loyalty and ask for referral business*
4. *Respond fast*
5. *Use a positive approach*
Others as they relate to you are – complete sheet according to your needs) . . .

- Of the above ideas, which one is likely to yield the best results for you?

- What percentage of sales (or performance) increase could realistically be expected?

- How long would it take:
  to develop the idea?
  to get results?

- Who would have to be involved?

- What date should you start?

- What is the first step you should take?

ACTION SECTION

1 Let yourself have a vision

Most psychologists agree that the vision comes before the creation. The sad part for many people is that they don't allow themselves to have vision. They block themselves before they have a chance to create it by thinking they can't have it.

Not Janet. She saw the travellers in the airport with luggage and she wanted to have it. She didn't say, 'Oh my parents are farm labourers, I'll never be able to have it.'

From all the motivation work I do with groups, I'm convinced that vision is one of the most critical factors of success. This is because it's the first step.

To have motivation to do something, you have to have a vision of what you want to achieve. You have to believe you can do it and you have to want it. But without the vision, there is no creation.

What visions have you been blocking? We each have visions coming into our heads which are different from anyone else's visions. Perhaps there's a reason for it.

Why not let your visions roll before putting a damper on them? Then you can use them as Janet did to create your own future.

2 Tell the truth

A big issue in Janet's business is price. Janet's philosophy is that if customers know the cost of the product and the amount of her commission, their negotiation attitude will be better.

What's the big issue in your business? If your customers knew the truth about it, would it improve their attitude? Try it and see. The results might surprise you.

3 Get their loyalty and ask for referral business

'When I deliver the car to you, if you find my service is good, please refer business to me,' says Janet. Then she goes on to tell them exactly what she expects.

Janet is loyal to her customers. She goes out of her way to do favours for them. She doesn't do the bare minimum. She spends her own time and money off the job on them. She doesn't think they'll mind doing her a favour in return.

What do you do to build loyalty? Will your customers mind giving you referral business in exchange? If you're not up to 60 per cent referral business yet, as Janet is, why not try asking for it rather than assuming you'll get it. 'Ask and ye shall receive.'

4 Respond fast

Part of the loyalty Janet builds is through fast response. Her customers know she really cares. She makes herself accessible with a pager and by encouraging them to call her at home. She responds fast to their phone calls, spending three to four hours a day on the telephone. The results pay off handsomely.

What steps can you take to respond fast to your customers? Put the shoe on the other foot. Think about how good it feels when someone returns your call in five or ten minutes rather than hours or days later. It makes you feel good. It builds your loyalty.

5 Use a positive approach

Janet uses a positive approach in sales and in everything in her life. 'Very good car,' she says, when they see a car they like.

Enthusiasm – a positive approach – is contagious. It acts like a magnet, drawing people towards it. Dale Carnegie, whose human relations courses span the world, said 'Think enthusiastic and you'll be enthusiastic'.

Janet steers away from negativity because she knows it repels people. Even when they have an awful trade-in she says, 'Not so bad . . . I'll try to give you the best price.'

People need encouragement. They don't need more people telling them what is wrong with their business, the community, the world, and politics. They hear enough of that from other people. If you want to be an outstanding success in sales or anything in your life, take a tip from Janet. Let all the words that flow from your lips and mind be positive. Start today.

CHAPTER THREE

The Love of the Challenge

"No glory without guts"

BOB BROADLEY

Australia
National Mutual Insurance

After 15 years of hard work as a butcher, I wanted something easy to do. I decided on sales.

GIVE IT TO THEM STRAIGHT: USE SIMPLE LANGUAGE EVERYONE CAN UNDERSTAND

Bob Broadley believes in speaking in simple language which everybody understands. He made $770,000 in Australia that way last year, and $500,000 the year before, and $300,000 the year before that.

He puts his success down to his 15 years' experience as a butcher where he learned to deal with women. 'They pull 90 per cent of the purse strings', he says. Yet in Bob's field, insurance, he has to sell to both husband and wife, each with different techniques. His 95 per cent close rate means that he actually sells policies to 19 out of 20 couples he visits.

Equally as important is the fact that Bob doesn't rely on repeat business. Out of all the insurance he wrote last year, 60 per cent of it was to completely new clients.

Cold calling is something he has developed to perfection. 'I always make appointments with the husband,' says Bob. 'He needs to feel the commitment, but I usually sell to the wife. She knows the dollars and cents of their budget.'

SELL TO BOTH DECISION MAKERS

Selling to joint decision makers is one of the most difficult things salespeople face. Bob handles it by setting the atmosphere first and putting both parties at ease. If possible, he meets the clients in their home.

He prefers to talk over the kitchen table with coffee. With the kids in bed, the TV off.

His undying rule is to chat for a minimum of 10 minutes before talking business. 'I know the wife's reaction to the appointment will be: "Oh, no, not an insurance man." They need to feel they know me and I know them', he says.

His chat time usually includes positive feedback to the clients about their successes in life. 'I usually acknowledge the wife for her contribution to the family, because I don't believe women get credit for what they do often enough.' He typically says, 'Mrs Jones, if I can give you a compliment in front of your husband, it's lovely to walk into a clean home, you must work very hard.'

But, 'I don't say it if I don't mean it. If the house is a pigsty I talk about the children or other things that are important to them. Or I ask them what they did before their kids came along. I always tell the wives that their input is more important and that I'd like them to be there throughout our discussion.'

He feels it's vital to get the client involved. He makes them do their own number crunching on a calculator. If they don't have one, he lends them one.

PERFECT PROSPECTING: CHOOSE YOUR FAVOURITE GROUP FOR COLD CALLING

Bob doesn't believe in mixing social-life with business. He makes it a policy never to prospect friends or relatives unless they ask. Half of Bob's business comes from cold calling, eye to eye. His prospects are mainly self-employed people who are without income if they become sick, or have an accident. 'Skilled craftsmen are my favourite group', Bob says, 'They and their wives know how important it is to have income insurance protection.'

Bob has no qualms about cold calling. He'll walk right onto a construction site and say 'Good morning, Bob Broadley is my name. I'm talking to all you self-employed people in the area about non-cancellable accident and sickness insurance. I'm talking about money. If you can't work, who's going to feed you?'

He always talks to people in isolation, never more than two in a group. Brush-offs don't worry Bob because he knows he's got a product which can really benefit people. He's paid off a lot of sickness and death claims in his 16 years in insurance which helps him keep the benefit in his mind as he faces the brush-off.

PERFECT YOUR OPENING LINE

'I've got insurance, mate', they typically say. But Bob, who knows his competitors, says, 'Who with?' When he finds out, he pushes the strength of his policy against the weakness of the competition.

'Yea, it's cancellable,' Bob says. 'I know', says the prospect. 'I can cancel anytime I want.'

'No,' says Bob, 'I don't mean you, I mean the company.' Then he goes into a very graphic story with the prospect about friends who have had back injuries, were paid off, then dropped by the insurance company. 'With our policy, your friends would be fully insured until they were 65.' He's been using the same opening line for 16 years.

QUALIFY AFTER YOU WHET THEIR APPETITE

Then, when the customer's appetite is whet, he makes sure they are qualified to buy. 'Hang on Harry, you're a qualified tradesman, aren't you?' This technique makes the prospect feel almost lucky to be talked to. Bob's doing two things. One – building up the client's eagerness not to be rejected. Two – cutting his losses because the non-cancellable only covers qualified tradesmen.

Now, with the prospect enticed, he consolidates the appointment. 'All I want you to do is to compare it to what you have,' he says. He believes strongly in giving the prospect an out. 'All it will cost you is a few minutes and a cup of coffee.'

Coffee is an important selling tool, he believes, in creating a relaxed atmosphere. He also likes to feel it's a two-way street. They give something, he gives something.

SPEND 90 PER CENT OF YOUR TIME EITHER PROSPECTING FOR APPOINTMENTS OR BEING ON APPOINTMENTS

Bob values his time. 'If I'm not selling, I'm not doing my job.' His 12-hour days are spent face-to-face, either prospecting for appointments or at appointments. He feels that a major weakness of non-producing salespeople is that they think they are working when they are at the office. 'Paperwork doesn't get you business,' he says. By employing two people to handle the administrative side, he keeps his time more productive. And the investment pays off.

The first year Bob started in insurance, his only sales experience had been one year of selling coffee machines to factories. Before that, it had been 15 years of butchering. Nevertheless, in his first year of insurance he saw the importance of having back-up help. The coffee machine job paid him $20,000. His first year of insurance paid him $92,000, and so, six months into it, he took on a secretary to relieve him of the paperwork and release his time to sell.

GETTING THERE

His motto during his first year in insurance was to work, work, work. That meant 12-hour days, but it seemed like a holiday after 14-hour days in butchering. 'Getting into a shirt and tie just to talk to people seemed like retirement after the hard physical labour of butchering for 15 years. I loved it.'

Although he was good at maths, he was never fond of school. From the age of 14, when he left school, Bob started working at 4 a.m. at the butcher shop and finished at 6 p.m. At 12 he had found his first job learning to sell ice cream as a 'lolly boy' in a cinema. He worked his way up to the circle where he knew that young men were willing to spend more money on their dates.

In fact, he earned so much money working four nights a week and Saturdays, that he surpassed his tax-free earning limit and was the first 'lolly boy' to pay tax.

So we see, again, that high expectations come early in life. Determination and faith in himself got Bob back into sales after butchering. He wanted to try something easier and decided on sales, but no one would hire him without experience. Finally, at the ninth interview, he said, 'Look, before you reject me, let me work for three months without pay to prove myself.'

That takes guts for a man in his 30s with a wife and three kids to support. But Bob's a person who takes responsibility for his own future. He knew what he wanted, and it wasn't butchering.

IF YOU'RE IN MANAGEMENT, DO YOU SUPPORT INNOVATIVE IDEAS?

His first week on the new job with the coffee machine company showed his persistence. The other four reps sold an average of one machine per month. Bob wanted to quadruple that. He saw that the only way was to put the machine in on a free trial basis. He reasoned that, if the secretaries got used to the ease of using them, with no cups to wash up, they wouldn't let the machine go at the end of the week.

His management wouldn't support the idea, so Bob laid out $1,200 from his own pocket to buy three machines. Remember, this man was on zero salary, had a family to support, and was again showing his determination.

He put the machines on tree trial and sold them all within the week. His sales record was now 12 times the average and he increased it to six machines per week, 24 times the average. A few months later, management adopted his free trial policy!

It proves the point that high performers don't wait for management to see the light.

After nine months in the coffee machine business he made a call to an insurance company. 'You're wasting your time in coffee machines, son, get into insurance,' said the manager.

'You've got to be kidding,' thought Bob. 'Like everyone else, my opinion of insurance salesmen left something to be desired.'

But the manager was persistent. He haunted Bob *and* his wife for three months, and the rest is history.

In his first year on the job he ranked second in the league table, earning $92,000 when the average was $10,000, against people with 20 years' experience.

In his second year he achieved his most memorable form of recognition. It was a letter from the General Manager, congratulating him on his achievement. 'To attain an annual net production of $4,000,000 in such a short period is *without parallel*,' it said.

Now Bob's house is filled with plaques of acknowledgments of all descriptions – even gold and marble. But he still points to that first letter in a humble black frame as his most meaningful accolade.

LIFESTYLE: BALANCE YOUR HOME AND BUSINESS LIFE

Balancing family and work has always been a priority for Bob. 'The kids never saw me in the evenings when they were young, but I compensated by working only Monday through Thursday. On Friday I went into the office for two hours of paperwork, then took my wife to lunch and called it quits for the weekend.'

His son Dean is now 22, Stuart 18 and daughter Donna, who works in the business, 20.

Even now he views his three-day weekend as sacred. I visited Bob at his 23-acre estate in Warrandyte, just outside Melbourne. Looking out of the floor-to-ceiling glass windows in all directions, one is struck with the tranquillity which Bob has strived hard over the years to create.

An indoor swimming pool, jacuzzi and pool-table room, plus the tennis court and *two* four-car garages give you an idea how the money Bob earns is put to use.

He and his wife, Maree, have also invested in property. From six years ago with their own home, a butcher shop, and a three-unit apartment building, they've increased their holdings substantially. They now own three engineering factories, a commercial property on two acres which they subdivided, an office building with shops and an office block in the heart of Melbourne. The office block, they say, was their first big gamble. The $3 million building had an outgoing of $450,000 per year and only one tenant when they purchased it. But risk-taking is something they both enjoy.

I asked Bob how he handles his new-found wealth and also if he noticed a difference in the way people treated him.

'Well, I called a wood craftsman the other day. When he arrived he said "I charge $60 an hour". I said, "Oh yeah, what would you charge if I didn't have a house like this?" Then I said, "Never mind, you're a professional, aren't you? Tell me about your accident and sickness insurance, is it cancellable or non-cancellable?" '

Can you guess the rest. The woodwork is done and the craftsman has a new insurance policy!

Whether it's property or insurance, Bob is not the type to rest on his laurels. Shortly after starting in insurance, his goal was to retire as a millionaire at 40. He achieved it, 'barely' Bob says modestly, but it only lasted three weeks. 'I walked around golf courses thinking how much money I was losing by not working and, anyway, I was getting beat at golf and couldn't stand it,' he says.

So back to work he went. Today, even with the $770,000 commission, he's looking for new ways to increase sales. He sees a big market in accountants and solicitors.

One of Bob's big philosophies is 'Know your product, know your product.' So he's back to school two hours a week with six hours of homework for 14 weeks. 'You have to be able to explain everything the customer wants to know – you have to shoot the answer.' This, he says, gives him credibility and builds trust with the client.

DROP THE JARGON

Even with the man on the street he is careful to explain everything, simply and carefully. 'If they don't understand, they won't buy,' he says, 'I could say, I'm going to give you a "triple term policy", but I don't. I say "I'm going to keep the cover premium level for ten years for you." Straight is best. You have to understand it yourself before you can explain it.'

Bob also believes in being honest. 'Fair Dinkum', as some of his Australian clients call it. 'I look right in their eyes and say, "I'm going to make some money for myself and I have something worthwhile for you." They respect you for that.'

Running out of challenges seems to be the drawback I could detect for Bob. In the early days he struggled with cold calls and converted one person in 30 talked to into an appointment. Now it's one in five. That's a 600 per cent improvement. What's the difference? Not taking 'no' for an answer. 'Now I know the questions to ask, so I don't take no for an answer.' Prospects who say they have insurance, but can't remember the company, now get more probing. 'If I think they're lying, I go back to my honesty policy – "I'm going to make myself some money and I have something worthwhile for you. All it will cost you is 15 minutes and a cup of coffee."' Away he goes.

And he's not put off by the four out of five who don't materialize into an appointment. 'I'm happy because I know I'm closer to the fifth – the one who says yes.' And I thought he meant it!

What about lame excuses from the prospect? Because Bob sees both husband and wife, his appointments have to run straight through dinner time. 'Oh but you can't come at dinner time,' Bob often hears. He counters that with 'That's fair enough, Harry, that's my dinner time, too. Do you mind asking your wife to put it back half an hour?' He says he's never been refused once with that reply. And he *never* leaves business cards when fixing up the appointment. He believes, when they don't have his number, they don't cancel.

THE THREE-PART MAGIC

I spent a long time talking with Bob and comparing his techniques to others around the world. He insists that his success lies in being a strong closer.

Yet, I think he's too modest. What I saw coming through were three strong stages of his sales technique, all vital to success. To earn $770,000 in commission he has to be doing everything to perfection.

What I saw first was his prospecting. To win one appointment in five conversations is superb in this business. And to do it relentlessly year after year for 60 per cent of your business is phenomenal.

Secondly, I saw that he gets both decision makers together on the first call and he won't talk if one or other is out of the room. Therefore he eliminates call-back excuses.

HAVE SOLID CLOSING QUESTIONS

Thirdly, he closes, and he closes hard. After his presentation he asks five straightforward closing questions:

1. Do you want to save income tax? The biggest mistake, Bob advises, is to answer for the prospect. 'Never, never, never say, "Of course you do."' The *client* must answer. Then he waits. He just waits and waits. Once he counted to 30. Then he repeated the question. Later he discovered the reason. The poor prospect hadn't filed a tax return for five years and was afraid he'd report him.
2. Can you afford the premiums? Talk to the wife. Wait for the answer.
3. Do you feel you need the death coverage? Wait.
4. Do you think when Harry gets to 55 you'll need the money? Harry is self-employed, no one will give him anything.
5. How would you like to pay, monthly or yearly?

The closing includes handling objections as if they didn't exist. 'We want to talk to our accountant', they might say.

'What do you want to talk to your accountant for?' Bob asks. 'Do you believe it's tax deductible? OK, then I'm sure you don't ask him how many bottles of beer or how much groceries to buy. This has nothing to do with an accountant.'

These simple analogies seem to work magic for Bob. An analogy can't be thought up for every objection. Practice and conviction make them stick.

Rejection is a major problem for salespeople. Bob believes nine out of ten sales reps get too embarrassed over rejection. 'I love cold calling face-to-face. I love rejection because I know I'm closer to the one saying "yes".'

REFLECTION

As Bob drove me back to Melbourne from his beautiful estate, I reflected on his enthusiasm. I wondered how he manages to keep it up, year after year. So I asked him.

'Bob, what's the hardest thing about the business?' 'It's to do it constantly, year after year,' was his reply.

'And what would you do differently if you had life to live over again?' 'I'd pace life out better. I'd spend more time with my wife and kids. When I think back now to my children, I probably had four week-night meals with them in their lives.'

'Not so bad,' I said. 'What about all those three-day weekends, year after year, doesn't that count?' I asked. 'Yea, but I often think how time flies. You can't replace that time with the kids once they grow up,' he said.

'What advice would you give others about success?' I asked.

'Dedication – that's first – give it 100 per cent. Second, be honest, that's important. Third, it takes sweat. I've never met a millionaire who hasn't worked darn hard.'

'Bob, what is the most fun for you in this job?'

'Well I love challenge,' he answered. 'I guess it's when people say "*You can come in but we're not going to buy anything tonight.*" '

'How soon they learn', I thought.

ACTION SHEET

Use this sheet, and the action section which follows, to enhance your own sales techniques and achievements.

Ideas for development:
1. *Give it to them straight: use simple language everyone can understand.*
2. *Sell to both decision makers.*
3. *Perfect prospecting: choose your favourite group for cold calling.*
4. *Spend 90 per cent of your time either prospecting for appointments or being on appointments.*
5. *If you're in management, do you support innovative ideas?*
6. *Lifestyle: balance your home and business life.*
7. *Have solid closing questions.*
Others as they relate to you are – (complete sheet according to your needs)

• Of the above ideas, which one is likely to yield the best results for you?

• What percentage of sales (or performance) increase could realistically be expected?

• How long would it take:
to develop the idea?
to get results?

• Who would have to be involved?

• What date should you start?

• What is the first step you should take?

ACTION SECTION

1 Give it to them straight: use simple language everyone can understand

Bob believes in speaking in simple language everyone can understand. If this earns him $770,000 in commission, shouldn't we all listen to it?

Technical people often argue that when you use simple language you talk down to people. But I've never seen a sale lost yet because salespeople talked in understandable language.

Perhaps it would help to look at it this way. You can't possibly know the comprehension level of your prospect. By presuming you do know, you run the danger of talking above them. This creates mistrust. It loses the sale.

In our sales seminars, we have delegates list the benefits of their product (not the features). Then they exchange papers and answer 'yes' or 'no' to the following questions:

- Does the benefit tell what the customer gets?
- Is the benefit stated so that it is easy to understand?
- Is the benefit stated without using 'jargon'?
- Is the benefit stated in an enticing way? (Would you buy it based on this statement?)
- Think now of a way to state each benefit in a more convincing way.

Usually the benefit starts to fall apart at question 4, if not before. The truth is that the easier something is to understand, the more enticing it is. Prospects can then relate what you're talking about to their needs.

Why not develop a benefit list according to the above criteria? Attendees of our seminars report at least a 40 per cent increase in sales from learning to talk 'benefit' in a simple, straightforward, understandable way. What percentage increase could you expect? Is it worth the effort?

2 Sell to both decision makers

Bob gets both decision makers together on the first call. This saves call backs. This also ensures that they hear the same thing. Then one person doesn't come up with objections which negatively influence the other.

How hard is it to get two or more decision makers together? It may be tough, but consider the fact that Bob closes 19 out of 20 prospects seeing both decision makers together. What steps can you take to:

- find out who all the decision makers are before you present?
- get them into one room together before you present?
- acknowledge them all for their influence on the decision?

The result might be the difference between doing 19 out of 20 sales or one out of 20.

What percentage increase in sales could you expect? What can you do to ensure both/all decision makers are there?

3 Perfect prospecting: choose your favourite group for cold calling

Bob has identified skilled craftsmen as the group who most need his product and the group he's most comfortable with. His opportunities are endless. He never flinches at the thought of cold calling. He has perfected a strategy which works.

What group needs your product most? Are you comfortable working with them? Answering these questions could yield enormous results for you.

4 Spend 90 per cent of your time either prospecting for appointments or being on appointments

Bob thinks that people kid themselves into thinking they are working when they are not. Paperwork doesn't get you business and, although it is a necessary evil in all businesses, the question is one of emphasis.

Sometimes as salespeople we have to confront ourselves. Are you avoiding that cold call? If so, why not learn how to do it better with a group you like.

Are you in a friendly supportive environment at the office? Maybe so, but it won't make you money. What motivation techniques do you need to use to get yourself out in the field 90 per cent of the time?

What techniques do you need to get yourself on the phone? What works for many people is to get organized ahead: have all the phone numbers ready, all the addresses planned. Then you can move quickly through them.

Another technique people use is to treat themselves when they finish a list of tasks. A quick lunch at a favourite place, a friendly phone call. Whatever works for you. What steps can you take?

5 If you're in management, do you support innovative ideas?

Chances are that there are ideas out there which could quadruple your sales.

Bob's management wouldn't support his idea of putting coffee machines into companies on a trial basis. Because of his determination, Bob laid out his own $1,200, and increased sales by 24 times the average.

Some managers are so afraid of change that they miss out on opportunities and lose good people.

Tom Peters[1] says in his book, *Thriving on Chaos*, that you need to sit down at the end of the day and ask yourself what *changes* you've made today to meet your changing business environment.

What was the last idea put to you? How did you respond? If you cut the person off too shortly, you may have lost a golden opportunity. What can you do to stimulate new ideas while limiting the risk?

6 Lifestyle: balance your home and business life

I remember hearing about a professor of engineering who told his university class, 'Remember not to sell your soul to your company. When you drop dead from a heart attack, the company will replace you the next day.' There's probably some truth in that.

How do you balance your home and business life? 'Kids grow up too fast,' stresses Bob. 'You can't replace that time with the kids once they grow up.'

Are you getting the balance you want? If not, it won't come later by accident. It needs to be programmed into your schedule *now*.

Where do you stand on the balance scale? Could a change give you more satisfaction now and in the long term?

What steps can you take now?

7 Have solid closing questions

Look at Bob's five closing questions. Some people think selling is mystical. It's not. It's a step-by-step process. Bob's questions progress the sale steadily.

- Do you want to save tax? Yes. (Reinforcing benefit.)
- Can you afford the premiums? Yes. (Overcoming the most common objection.)
- Do you feel you need the coverage? (Confirming need and getting commitment on first grounds.)
- Do you think you'll need the money? (Confirming need and getting commitment on second grounds.)
- How would you like to pay, monthly or yearly? (Assumptive and alternative close wrapped into one.)

What closing questions can you use to lead your prospect step by step to a decision and increase your sales?

[1]Macmillan 1988

CHAPTER FOUR

Sales and Production – the Twain *Shall* Meet

"One can never know too much"

MICHELINE NOTTEBOOM DUSSELIER
Belgium
Manufacturing – Export sales through distributors
AXXIS, DSM Dutch State Mines

Production and sales can be two conflicting departments. I try to match their interests, so that they both meet the company's goals.

Micheline Notteboom came on board as the only woman in sales at the AXXIS & NV, a member of the ERTA Group, and subsidiary of DSM (Dutch State Mines). The company started practically from scratch, winning business from established manufacturers in the industry.

Now, at 29, she travels through Europe heading export sales and has whacked away at her three major foreign competitors.

'Prior to joining AXXIS, my ambition was to be a secretary in a top position.' She achieved that early in life and then looked for greener pastures.

'I wanted a job in which I could use more of my own initiative,' she said. So with the encouragement of her husband and brother, who were both in sales with jobs she saw as having higher challenge and authority, she took the leap.

She applied for a job in 'inside sales', and she got it. That was in 1984. Although she's modest about saying so, she was able to remarkably increase her salary, and has continued to make steady progress. Now she heads export which is 90 per cent of the company's 500 million Belgian franc turnover.

'But I don't regret my administrative background,' she said. 'I learned a lot that I use today from my boss.' He was Vice President of Corporate Strategy of the ERTA Group Management which oversaw six companies within the group in those days.

SET HIGH STANDARDS

'I became involved in the problems we had. This included the strategy, the cost control, the sales and the marketing situation of six diverse companies. That taught me a lot.' And most of all Micheline had a role model in her boss – a man who had the highest of reputations among clients.

'I had a choice when I went into my own sales career. I could take the easy road of a non-perfectionist to keep the office staff happy, or the road of high standards like my boss did, and keep the clients happy.'

She chose the high standards route, and hasn't looked back since.

Her customers, the distributors she sells to, have this to say about her: 'She gives every possible help to make us successful,' said one. 'She reacts to problems promptly.'

'This doesn't mean she takes decisions without thinking them through. She never takes a decision that she regrets later.'

'She is very responsible and she always tries to find a way to satisfy both her company and the distributor.'

'She is extremely thorough. If we have problems that are not directly her company's fault, they will do everything to help. The whole company is that way.'

'She is always giving us ideas on how to confront the competition.'

TRUST

Another distributor said, 'She is not a person who would sell you 100 items if you need 99. With Micheline you never have to worry, it's like dealing with your family. We have a warm and personal relationship with her. Whenever we have a problem, she's there to help. She doesn't pull the wool over your eyes, she only deals in facts.' Truthfulness was something he stressed more than once.

STYLE

Another said, 'She can be extremely persistent. She will always come back to the point she wants to go over. She is very forceful in her presentation and the way she sees the facts.'

'She's very experienced and we benefit from that a lot. She makes you realize that she's part of the company's team and she sets a good example.'

Wouldn't we all like to have commendations such as these! Much of Micheline's style today goes back to the success techniques she learned from her early boss. She remembers how meticulous he was. 'Typing with errors came back with big red lines through it. I learned not to do things halfway. It's all or nothing for the customer.'

And she learned organization – everything from filing systems to follow up, to organizing client visits. 'I saw the results of this extraordinary planning and forethought. Everything that might happen and could happen was thought through.'

Today she uses this planning with customers to get her own results. 'Everything has to be arranged before a client visit, from pick-up, to the meeting, to the entertainment, to seeing them off.'

Afterwards, she writes to the customer to review the key points of the meeting, the action points agreed by each side and the actions, if any, taken so far. She does this after every meeting whether at home or abroad and distributes it to those concerned.

We asked Micheline what advice she would give a new person just starting out who wanted to be a success in any field. Her answer was: 'Avoid misunderstandings by verifying that your message was received clearly and vice versa.'

Despite this, Micheline is still amazed at how often people forget what was discussed and agreed. 'Telling people things once just doesn't seem to be enough.'

A technique she finds helpful is to start meetings with a review. She often says, for example, 'Remember at the last meeting we talked about setting new targets and I confirmed these in writing. Now I'd like to start where we left off and . . .' This focuses people's minds and helps them remember.

The success techniques she uses get tremendous results for AXXIS. 'No one expected us to come on so strong in such a short time,' she says. They now turnover 500 million Belgian francs compared with 465 million the year before, and 350 million the year before that.

Their increase in the market has been more than double that of anyone else in the industry.

How has she managed to enter into her competitors' market so forcefully? Micheline puts much of her success down to her understanding of production.

In her industry delivery is the most critical aspect of building a customer base. 'When the customer needs a product, they usually need it now. They can't afford to wait for a supplier who has a backlog in production and a long delivery period.'

Micheline's company makes plastics which are 800 times tougher than glass. They're used for everything from telephone cabins to windows. You see them used for police riot shields, transparent panels in shopping centres and railway stations.

USE YOUR FLEXIBILITY TO BREAK INTO NEW MARKETS

'From the first moment we started the company, I put pressure on the production side,' she says. 'We looked at the strength of our competitors and we talked to customers. We saw an advantage in being small. We had flexibility and could deliver faster.'

Therefore, much of the way she's broken into the market is to offer better service overall and particularly on small non-standard orders.

'It takes about a year,' she says, 'to build up their trust. Then, when we prove our track record of supply and service consistently, they are willing to place the large standard orders too.'

But, even now, the stress is on production. 'One potential order', she said, 'was about 15 tons and had to be manufactured, cut to size, packaged, shipped abroad and delivered on site within six days.'

Knowing the stress on production, she talked with the distributor ahead, weighed up the likelihood of getting the order, and reserved half of their production space on spec. She knew the end user, had visited his overseas site, and had delivered ten smaller orders over the previous year. It was a gamble which, had it backfired, would not have helped her credibility in her company.

But it's the liaison between sales and production which Micheline stresses as the reason for her own, and the company's, success. 'If I have a particular project for an important client which has a tight delivery schedule, I go straight to our own production people. I know our entire future credibility lies in delivering on time,' she says.

If she's 70 per cent sure she'll get the order, she gets the commitment of production before accepting. 'The chances are 70 per cent that we'll get this job. If we get it, can you guarantee me that we can do it?' she says to them. But she doesn't stop there. If she gets a 'yes', she asks, 'Can I have your commitment before I say "yes".'

I listened with some scepticism because I know how difficult it is liaising between production and sales.

'What happens when you get a "no"?' I asked. 'Do you always try to talk them into it?'

I presumed she would, but I was only half right. 'Yes and no,' was her answer. 'I always go back to discuss it,' she says. 'I might say, "This is a very important order. It's an exceptional contract. We have to organize ourselves so we can do it."'

But that's not enough. Many production departments in companies hear that from salespeople every day. What makes her successful?

'I go out of my way to understand the production process,' she says, 'So when I tell them how important the order is, I can also discuss the possibilities and limitations of production.'

She can discuss with them the hassle they have to face by changing the production sequence. She can sympathize with them about their loss of production efficiency. 'If I ask for a change in sequence,' she says, 'it will be a problem in the weekly sequence, which can even extend to the monthly sequence. It will mean a rescheduling on paper and a change in raw materials feed-in. It will mean resetting all the machines and changing all preparatory work.'

Who can resist being swayed by such compassion? One of Dale Carnegie's golden rules I remember is: 'To win people to your way of thinking, see things from their point of view.'

USE PERSISTENCE WITHIN THE COMPANY

Micheline has obviously mastered the rule. The same persistence and sales skill she uses with her customers comes through inside the company. Having won their support, she can now offer suggestions. 'Can we change the sequence partially to reduce disruption and still get the order out?' she asks.

She insists on trying out angles to make it work. But when it's all said and done, if she's convinced that the profit from the order would not compensate for the loss from the disruption, she drops it. And so she keeps herself and others focused on the company's best interest.

Why don't more salespeople learn to liaise with production more often, as Micheline does? It seems so basic, so fundamental to success.

Is it lack of time and effort? Is it lack of management backing to encourage the liaison?

Some might say it works because they are a small company of 45 people. But not so. Micheline's husband, she tells me, works for a large, market-leader company in textiles with much larger production apparatus. The liaison between production and sales works in much the same way despite more complicated production changes. Perhaps more companies should rethink production flexibility to meet competitive challenges.

Then salespeople could have the backing of management. But their need for commitment is also important. They must want to learn about production. Micheline, for example, attends production seminars whenever possible. And she focuses her energy on liaison between departments. When I asked what priority she placed on targeting her energy, she listed as follows: first the production supervisor, second the sale assistant, third the shipping and packing department.

Isn't that interesting? A top performer in sales and she focuses half or more of her internal energy on non-sales personnel. This happens mainly when she has to change the production schedule, which is about 25 per cent of the time.

But, what about outside the company? What makes Micheline's style work where others fail?

SUPPORT THE DISTRIBUTOR WITH TARGETS

As all of us who work with distributors know, keeping them motivated to concentrate on your product is not an easy job.

I asked Micheline how she handled setting their targets. 'We set targets each year and revise them each half year,' she said. 'Then we have quarterly reviews.

'The most important thing is following up the distributor after the target is agreed upon. Is it being carried out? If not, why not? Perhaps the competitors have had a price change, a general policy change with regard to distribution, or even an extension to their total package of products.'

She gives them constant support on competitive information and together they decide how to tackle changes country by country, area by area.

In addition to setting distributors targets, she also sets market sector targets by types of end user. These, too, get filtered down to distributors. The more precisely you know your targets, the better you can track your success or make necessary changes of strategy to meet your overall growth target.

What about conflict between distributors? These are inevitable in markets in which several distributors operate.

Micheline and her company like to be honest and open. They feel it's vital to quote the same price to two people bidding on the same job. Yet in all situations one distributor is prepared to give it more effort than another depending on the time and circumstances. In this case their extra support goes to the one willing to make the extra effort.

MAKE THE EXTRA EFFORT

What does Micheline see as ways to motivate distributors?

First is *trust*. She has a philosophy of partnership with their distributors. 'They have to see you take personal care,' she stresses.

Second is *support*. Your distributor must feel sure that his enquiry will be answered by a person who:

a) knows the product;
b) knows the competitive situation in his country;
c) knows how his company operates, his goals, problems and so on.

Third is *confidence* in the company's future growth. The distributors need to know that you are working on product development, quality and all areas of your business that will help them.

As far as personal motivation of distributors goes, Micheline pays close attention to putting together a good agenda before each meeting. She says that the results of the meeting will invariably come from one point or another on the agenda. Therefore, the better the agenda, the better the results!

Then she reviews the file for performance against target and makes a list of checkpoints for discussion. She always likes to bring, show or discuss one positive aspect he was not expecting. This could be:

• a piece of information related to his market.
• a proposal on documentation in the national language.
• a new development at AXXIS.
• a note of congratulations or a personal reward for performance or for getting a special project.

- a present or personal attention on a special occasion such as flowers at the inauguration of new facilities.

She finds that this helps to develop and consolidate relationships.

In fact Micheline says that her philosophy is to 'understand and discover the individual'. She says: 'I like to create an understanding of "give and take", and you can only do this by finding a mutual wavelength. I attach a lot of importance to the person I'm dealing with.'

She also has a philosophy which she calls 'knowing the finesses of things' whether they be situations, relationships or attitudes relating to her job. She handles this by:

- asking questions (either directly related or hypothetical).
- exchanging viewpoints.
- brainstorming.

Another way Micheline has supported her distributors was to have an international conference for the first time this year. 'Some manufacturers are defensive about getting their distributors together for fear they will talk about prices which are naturally different depending on volume,' Micheline says.

But she remains convinced that the motivational and educational aspects far outweigh any disadvantages. The response from distributors seems to back this up. One hundred per cent of them took up the invitation and paid their own airfare. Micheline's firm paid hotel accommodation and conference expenses.

'The event cost us 300,000 Belgian francs to run and we are projecting a 55 million Belgian franc increase in business from it!' Not a bad return on investment. She targeted her return based on the launch of a new product, plus doubling the turnover on another product.

'The key to success,' she says, 'is to use the conference to show them *how* to develop the market.' This includes showing them which market segments they can break into, using examples. She is careful to choose real examples which resulted in success for distributors. These will help them overcome problems.

'I always give case studies that are tried and tested,' she says. 'This gives your customer confidence and paints a mental picture of how he can follow it with the same success.'

In addition to telling them which markets to target, her examples include tips on how they can approach the new markets, and the problems they might encounter and overcome. 'They also exchange ideas on applications, and they leave with the enthusiasm and knowledge to increase sales. It's important, too, that they see how we are growing. We hope to double our capacity with our new extruder.' The conference has made an impact on how we plan to continue supporting them in the future.'

DEVELOP YOUR PERSONAL ORGANIZATION

What about personal organization? Again Micheline taps the wisdom gained from working with her previous boss, co-ordinating six companies within the group. 'I have a filing system which allows me to find anything within 15 seconds,' she boasts quite rightly. 'If it's not there, it's been misfiled by mistake.'

This time saving makes an enormous difference in Micheline's hectic life. It means that when she's ready to jump on a plane to any distributor, files are at her fingertips. This is important because her territory is widespread. It includes Italy, France, Belgium, UK, Ireland, Austria, Norway, Sweden, Denmark, Finland, Spain, Portugal and Greece.

It also means that she can grab a file when a client is on the line and instantly make him feel as though he's the most important person in the world (which he is, of course) by having his information at her fingertips.

Her filing system is broken down into four categories with subdivisions.

1. *Country files.* Within each country she has: sales leads; special projects; promotion; local competition; individual end users in major markets.
2. *Marketing files* including such things as: general market information; long-term business plan; short-term business plan; market research results; strengths and weaknesses; any figures on market share, turnover and organization.
3. *Product files* which include: delivery programme; specific applications; product development; specific technical information such as product classification according to national standards, eg British Standards, German DIN-Standards etc.
4. *Competitors' files.*

As we sat in the coffee lounge in Antwerp, where Micheline and I had our second meeting, I couldn't resist asking her some questions people often ask me.

'How do people react to you combining a high power career and marriage? Do they admire it? Or do they envy it?' I asked. 'How does it all affect your life?'

'Well, I remember when I was asked to take over export, it was quite a promotion but it meant travelling a lot. I knew this would have consequences for our home life as my husband also travelled a lot.

'I said to my boss, "I'm certainly interested. I'd like to think about it." I knew in my own mind that I wanted it. But I wanted to include my husband in the decision.'

When she did tell him, his reaction was, 'Of course, you're crazy if you don't take it.' This support clenched her enthusiasm for the sales promotion.

'That's one advantage of having similar careers.' They understand each other's problems and often talk after work about solutions. 'It's nice to have a good laugh about what happened at the office while preparing a light snack together in the evening.'

Micheline's husband, Patrick, is a solid soccer addict, having played in the first and second national division. Micheline is studying Swedish at night school which takes up one of the two nights that Patrick plays soccer. Otherwise, they wash up the dishes in time for the 7.45 Belgian news, watch comedies – their favourite is BBC's *Yes, Minister* – and then catch the *9 O'clock News* from England which comes on Belgian TV at 10.00.

What do others say? Well, many marvel at her hectic travel schedule, others find her job interesting, but can't quite grasp the complexity of it.

What about her credibility as a woman in the male world? 'I've never felt uneasy, even when I've been the only woman. I've never had any indication of not being accepted,' she says.

What technique does she use to create this environment? 'Firstly, I always act myself.' She thinks it's important to be natural. Most people see through a façade and it creates a barrier. 'Secondly, make sure this job is what you want to do; and thirdly, make face-to-face contacts as often as possible. It helps to create the atmosphere and build your relationships.'

And her bottom line axiom, which she attaches to everything at work, is to *respect deadlines on promises made.*

I can vouch for that. From day one my research assistant said, 'Watch this woman. She's answered every telex, fax and phone call exactly when she promised she would!'

The proverb she honours is 'Do not delay what you can do today.' A simple and swift road to the top!

ACTION SHEET

Use this sheet, and the action section which follows, to enhance your own sales techniques and achievements.

Ideas for development:
1. *Set high standards*
2. *Use your flexibility to break into new markets*
3. *Use persistence within the company*
4. *Support the distributor with targets*
5. *Develop your personal organization*
Others as they relate to your are − (complete sheet according to your needs)

- Of the above ideas, which one is likely to yield the best results for you?

- What percentage of sales (or performance) increase could realistically be expected?

- How long would it take:
  to develop the idea?
  to get results?

- Who would have to be involved?

- What date should you start?

- What is the first step you should take?

ACTION SECTION

1 Set high standards

Micheline modelled herself on an executive who was known as 'the best in the industry'. As a consequence, she has built a reputation for herself as being thorough, dedicated, persistent and forceful. At the same time she is well-liked and personable.

Success starts with the standards you set for yourself. Henry Ford said, 'If you think you can or you think you can't, you're always right. If you visualize yourself having high standards, chances are that you will.'

Many people back away from high standards because of the fear of the pressure that they might put on people. Micheline's boss sent back mistyped letters with big red lines through them. His team soon learned to do it right the first time. At the same time he gave them positive reinforcement for a job well done.

People do respond well to high standards if they have positive feedback on their performance.

What areas of your operation could use higher standards? What results could you expect? Who do you have to support to get these results? Is it worth it?

2 Use your flexibility to break into new markets

Micheline's company looked at the advantages they had to offer over the well-established competitors. They chose to offer non-standard products and to break into the market gradually. Once they established their credibility with customers, they could secure standard orders which undoubtedly would be more profitable.

This highlights a traditional conflict which often exists between profit margin and establishing a high market share at lower margins. Usually it costs more to produce non-standard orders. If it does, perhaps it's a trade-off to get your foot in the door and build a market presence which can be used later as a springboard. It's the vision that counts – the plan. Do you know where you're going and how you'll get there?

As David Campbell[2] said, *If you don't know where you're going, you'll probably end up somewhere else.'*

Where are you going? Can you use your flexibility to get there?

3 Use persistence within the company

This can be dangerous as well as useful. If you're not careful, you can become known as a pain in the 'you-know-what'.

But notice that when Micheline uses her persistence to get what she wants from the company for her customers, she does it from a position of

[2]Argus Communications, USA, 1974.

knowledge. She has taken the time to learn about production. While she's persistent, she also makes useful suggestions. She knows what objections to expect and brings them up ahead of time. 'It will mean changing this and changing that, but the results will be worth it.'

She's only persistent when she knows the profit from the order will compensate for the loss from the disruption to the company.

What areas could benefit from persistence within your company? Would a change be profitable? Can you overcome objections on the issue? Can you generate support for the idea?

4 Support the distributor with targets

'Targets won't work with our people.' Does that sound familiar? Bill Sykes and I hear it all the time from people who come on our sales and management seminars.

Yet after we cover the target section, they go away with targets for all parts of their companies and write to tell us about the tremendous results they achieve.

Targets relate to human nature. Remember at school, if you had a four-week deadline to do a term paper, you probably did most of it in the last four days. You probably could have done equally well in one week instead of four, with a dedicated effort.

The same is true in business. If you set monthly targets, you get results in one month. If you set weekly targets, you get results in a week. If you set no targets, you get results in an undefinable period.

When do you want results? Now, or in the undefinable period? The decision is yours.

Yes, it's hard to set targets for distributors. Nobody said life was easy. But dedicated professional distributors will know the value of targets as well as you do. The trick is to:

- Set the target *with* them, and
- Let them know from the beginning of the relationship what you expect, and put it in the contract.

If they don't want to participate, maybe they're not right for you.

Who can you support with targets? How will you implement this?

5 Develop your personal organization

Can you access any paper in your filing system in 15 seconds like Micheline does?

Can you do it while your customer is on the phone? If you could, would it help you become more efficient and make your life less hectic?

If a better system will help you, how will you motivate yourself to achieve it? Why not try the 'apple a day keeps the doctor away' system. Five minutes a day spent reorganizing files will work miracles in a two-week period.

CHAPTER FIVE

The Classic Sell

"My self development comes through people"

MICHAEL RENZ
Stuttgart
Automobile Sales, Mercedes Benz

The benefit to me of selling is that I've become more tolerant, more efficient by digging deeply into people's needs.

As I waited in London at Heathrow Airport for Michael Renz to arrive from Stuttgart for our interview, I wondered what a top Mercedes Benz salesman would look like. My research assistant had told me he'd be carrying a black pilot's case and wearing grey-rimmed glasses.

As everyone poured through immigration and passed through the exit doors I had a chance to examine them one by one. 'No, that one's too unkempt-looking. No, that one walks too aggressively. No, that one has the wrong image, too.'

I found myself looking for the classic IBM-type salesman – someone neatly dressed, someone exuding confidence in a non-aggresive sort of way. Someone of whom you would immediately say, 'There's a super guy. There's a winner.'

I wasn't disappointed. When Michael did arrive, I spotted him immediately. He was the only one of the 150 or so arriving passengers I'd scrutinized who fitted the part. Looking at him you said 'There's a person I can trust.' He had the classic look of success about him. As he spotted my white raincoat and looked up at me I had no hesitation in saying 'You must be Michael Renz'.

He had that pleasant, intelligent, highly presentable look that you expect from a top performer of one of the most prestigious companies in the world.

Over the next 21 hours of his visit, we had some of the most interesting discussions about sales that I've had the pleasure to indulge in.

I quickly discovered how he managed to make his reputation at Mercedes Benz. How he was able, in a two-year period, to take a difficult territory which was notoriously under average sales figures for Germany and accelerate the turnover 80 per cent.

No one before him had been able to do that, or even come close to it.

'The hardest part is converting customers to our product for the first time.' On a sales print-out produced by the company, I saw that Renz had an incredible record of converting these most difficult first-time buyers to choose a Mercedes.

In the employed sector of first-time buyers he was able to convert up to 110 per cent more buyers than the average salesperson. Of his total car sales, he sold 89 to first-time buyers, whereas the average was 44!

This is the most difficult sector to sell to. Repeat customers are easy by comparison. Once he converts a customer to Mercedes, they usually stay.

In fact he fondly remembers the easiest sale he ever made. He dropped in on a customer at his factory, as he normally does with all customers twice a year. After talking for barely half a minute the customer said: 'I want to buy a new car.' And he placed an order for his wife's car on the spot.

But it's not normally that easy. Renz says that he sees customers an average of five times from the point they start showing buying signals until the contract is signed.

He makes some 2,100 face-to-face visits each year. In the German system, salespeople go out to see the customer rather than vice versa. That's over eight visits per day. Coupled with his average record of 1,200 customers per year, he has achieved a reputation for top performance.

LINK BUYING NEEDS TO HUMAN NEEDS

Michael's style is classic with a depth of knowledge and sensitivity which is rare. He uses the stages of selling straight from the text book – the warm up, the customer needs analysis, the presentation, the closing.

But to this he adds his own profound thinking about what makes people tick. He quotes the psychologist Abraham Maslow and he links the buying motives of prospects to Maslow's pyramid of needs. 'People search to meet their needs or express themselves in all aspects of their lives,' he feels. 'If they don't get what they need in their youth, they try to find it later in life.'

And so, as he questions them about their requirements, he links it to the classic pyramid. If they imply the need for image or status, he links it to 'esteem needs', and he sells those features and benefits – the deep rich colour, the metallic paint, the alloy wheels.

If they imply they want safety, he links it to 'security'. If they prefer a light colour, he says 'It may not be fashionable, but it's safe'. He can then state the other safety features – the structure of the car, the airbag and so on.

Customers may have several levels of needs on the pyramid, but Michael believes one is always the strongest. He tries to find something to offer them which meets this strongest need. *Preferably he tries to find a feature which no one else can offer.*

He always keeps his presentation focused on their needs. It's like a mental game of chess. Question, question; answer, answer.

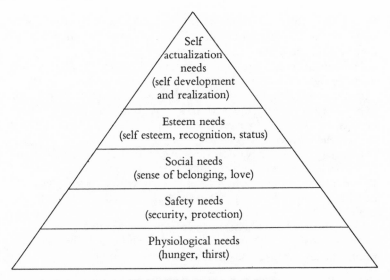

Maslow's hierarchy of needs

'The one who asks the questions sets the direction,' he emphasizes. 'I get information, then I repeat it. Then I ask another question which relates to the strategy.'

Repeating the customer's needs has two benefits: first, it reinforces the points; second, it gives him time to think of the next step of the strategy.

The strategy is to get all their needs out, repeat them, then deliver back exactly what you have that suits their needs.

If two people are buying, he finds their common and separate needs. Then he gives them a product which meets both their needs and has some extras for each. He makes sure by his communication that both people hear that their needs are being met.

separate need	common need	separate need

Selling to two people

MAKE THE DECISION THE CUSTOMER'S CHOICE

Even in selling to one person, it's essential that they make up their own mind and do not feel the sale is forced upon them. Michael sees himself largely as a person who puts the facts clearly for people in order to help them make a decision. 'People must have strong points of argument in order to make up their minds.' He is careful always to give them enough points so that they are absolutely sure of their decision.

He remembers one time making a fleet sale. After the decision was made by the manager and the contract signed, he spent a great deal of extra time with each sales rep who was to drive the car. Some salespeople may not have thought this necessary. But Renz wanted to get their conviction. 'If you try to operate without people's conviction, they will destroy the decision later'

He believes, 'If you buy or use anything it must be your own decision.'

As to why he feels this way he said, 'In our economy, compared to the Eastern bloc countries, we have freedom – freedom to buy, to influence our lifestyle. We lose our self respect if we don't make our own decisions.'

Self respect – a good phrase not to be forgotten in selling. Give it to the customer. Give it to yourself. When you both have it, the balance is right. You sell best when no one feels belittled or short changed. You are equals.

'I see a sales visit as an open discussion between friends,' says Renz. He claims never to have the feeling in the back of his mind that they *have* to buy a car. 'If it's your aim only to sell to the customer no matter what, your attitude and words will reflect that. You'll find yourself saying "That's the best car for you." This is a real mistake,' Renz professes.

Instead he says, 'If you take this and this point, what do you think is the best for you?' Naturally he gives enough evidence that the car meets the prospect's needs. Yet the decision is the prospect's.

Again Renz stresses that important aspect of freedom. The choice must be theirs. They must feel the conviction which comes mentally when they have to answer the question in their own mind rather than being 'sold to'.

When you ask the right questions, and give the right arguments for that person, the closing is easy. 'Let's fix these points we spoke about,' he might say. 'If we forgot something or you want to ask about my points we can do it now'

After the decision is finalized he revalidates the customer's decision. Such statements as, 'You made a good decision – you wanted security, you have that. You have status, too. The colour you chose and the upholstery are in good taste. The decision was the best possible one.'

Then Michael thanks the customer for his trust.

To have a good closing, you have to have a good opening.

The right opening has to set the scene for no pressure. 'If you have the freedom to choose the car you like, what things are important to you?' he asks as an opening question.

I asked Michael how he felt this question was different from a shorter form of the same question, 'What things are important to you?'

'It's a subtle difference,' he said. 'The first part of the sentence gives the customer a feeling of not being "sold to".' They might even talk about what they like about other cars which helps Michael find out what needs they have.

The second form would restrict their response. The first question forces them towards giving you more details which are meaningful to them.

TAKE RESPONSIBILITY FOR ACCURATE COMMUNICATION

From this discussion you can see that communication is something Michael focuses on. He sees it as an important part of success in business and in personal life. 'Let's say I say something,' he told me. 'Now you receive it according to all your past experiences. In other words, it goes through your filter.

'I have to be responsible that you hear it the way I mean it. If you don't eventually understand it the way I mean, it's my fault.'

He always tries to give feedback, such as, 'If I hear you correctly . . .' or 'Let's review what we've agreed . . .' and he repeats what the customer said.

In his sales calls he tries to make his communications 'perfect'. He leaves a sales call and he says to himself, 'Michael, you have to try to do it better.' If something went wrong, he asks himself what it was. Invariably he finds a mistake in not feeding information back to the prospect correctly or often enough. 'You must never presume anything. You must listen fully,' he stresses.

'More than 50 per cent of the time', he estimates, 'there are communication differences in some part of the sales process! This usually happens in either the needs analysis or the response to the needs.

'You have to correct these and then go to the next steps.'

I sat in awe listening to Michael talk about wanting to be 'perfect' in communication. When you reflect on the problems of corporations, the problems of people and the problems of the world, you know that communication is a major factor. Here's a man whose goal is to transcend that of mere mortals, to 'perfect his communication'.

What drives a person like this? Not just to achieve excellence in sales, but to develop *himself* to the highest heights.

I asked Michael why he chose sales as a profession. His answer was self development. He said that he saw science as too narrow. Although his education was scientific, he saw the possibility of self-development through working with people. 'The benefit to me,' he says, 'is that I've become more tolerant, more efficient by digging deeply into people's needs. Formerly, I couldn't feel so deeply,' he says.

He says that this helps him in all aspects of his life and he quotes his relationship with his four-year-old daughter as a case in point. One evening she asked him if he remembered being in kindergarten. With a few compassionate questions he was able to discuss her fear of changing schools after they moved to Stuttgart from Nuremberg. When she discovered that he had had similar experiences she became very positive in her attitude. 'If people have a problem, and they know others do, too, it changes their attitude. They see it as normal and they develop confidence in handling it,' says Michael.

He uses the same listening, probing and feedback skills with her that he has developed with clients. Now he listens, talks with her about her impressions of the day and finds out what her deep impressions are. Before, he used to focus on what he thought his response should be with people rather than using his energy to understand their needs.

OBJECTIONS – MENTALLY WALK WITH THEM, NOT AGAINST THEM

He uses this same sensitivity in handling objections. 'Customers can be influenced by other people who put an objection in their mind,' he says. 'Perhaps they go to their Stammtisch – the restaurant where they meet their friends on a weekly basis. Then their friends may talk up the advantages of a competitive car over the Mercedes.'

Now Michael's work starts again. But instead of launching straight into the virtues of the Mercedes, he takes time to sympathize with the customer's objections.

They may come back to him and say, 'The image of the other car is newer, it's in, the design is better.'

Michael sympathizes, 'Yes, if you take that point in the design – the front, for example – you see the double headlights. It looks dynamic, it looks almost aggressive. It looks sporty.' He's still sympathizing with the prospect's objection.

I asked Michael how long he felt it necessary to sympathize. 'Until I've confirmed that I understand him and I have validated his objection,' was the answer. 'Until we have reached a common understanding of the problem.' To demonstrate his point, he walked across the room with his arm held out as if leading a person along the path. 'You have mentally to walk in the direction of the customer's objection, arm-in-arm. Then, when they are convinced you see their point of view, you can turn them around. Then you are in the lead.'

'When do you change directions?' I asked. 'When you feel it's right,' he said. To quantify it better, he estimated that he spent about five per cent of the total presentation time 'walking' in the direction of the objection.

When the moment to turn around comes, he uses the same argument the customer had in favour of how competition met his need, but this time in favour of *his* product.

The presentation continues like this: 'Let's take the example of design you just mentioned. I want to show you the way we did it and the way the competitors did it. Then you'll see what your advantage is.' *Notice how he points out the benefit to the customer of listening to his explanation.* This is the moment he turns the customer around.

'If you take the car and it's design, it's fashionable. Maybe it's OK for today. But I know you plan to keep your car for five to ten years and you'll want to have a modern car then, too. Mercedes has classic designs which maintain style and value.'

The end result is that he's used the customer's own argument about having a new-looking car to prove an argument 'for', not 'against', his product.

Then he moves on to the advantage he can offer based on previous discussions. If the advantage is value, he shows that for equivalent miles driven, his car maintains 74 per cent of the basic price as opposed to 63 per cent by the competitive car over a three-year period.

If the advantage is security, he shows how his product exceeds government standards. 'Whereas many government crash tests use a wall which is wider than the width of the car for head-on crash tests, most accidents involve only 40 per cent of the front of the car or less. Our cars are built to withstand that 40 per cent offset test. In fact we build cars to withstand three times as many different tests as are legally required.'

Then he moves on to what advantages his car alone can offer, such as ASR which offers maximum traction and safety within physical limits, even though the driver accelerates on ice. He also mentions other specifics to meet the customer's security needs.

And so the classic sale goes:

- Start with setting the atmosphere.
- Get the needs.
- Present arguments which meet the needs.
- Close the sale.

And, in the process, verify the communication and overcome the objections. Validate the customer's self esteem and keep up your own self esteem and motivation.

RECHARGE YOUR SELF ESTEEM

Sounds easy, doesn't it? Yet we know it's not. We may know the right thing to do, but how do we motivate ourselves to do it?

Michael thinks that motivation and self esteem are essential aspects of success and again he links it to the Maslow pyramid of success.

If you go back to the pyramid, you'll see 'esteem needs' near the top: 'self esteem, recognition, status'. Leading up to it are 'social needs': 'sense of belonging, love' – of self and others. What actually makes us succeed or fail with our own motivation and esteem?

Michael reiterates the thoughts of philosophers and gurus throughout the ages: it's all in the mind. 'We all have pressures that are hard to face.' He cites an example: 'Let's say I have a very heavy schedule and my manager comes in to give me one more task. My mind at that moment wants to escape. It tells me I need to be on holiday or anywhere else than here. Then it's up to me to get a grip on it and realize I will only enjoy the holiday after the hard work is finished.'

He also feels it's essential to learn to deal with negativity which is an inescapable part of our environment. This is especially true in sales where rejections and objections abound.

To overcome it, he tries to focus on the advantages he can offer his customers. His sympathetic nature, his friendliness and his conscientiousness are all qualities he knows he has which he uses to overcome his feelings of being down.

When he's had a bad day, he finds it's better to 'clear the air' of his mind rather than let it brood. He often takes a walk in the forest and thinks the situation through step by step. 'I went in good, I came out bad – what went wrong?' he asks himself.

He goes through the day looking at his agenda, finds the point where it went wrong and then analyses it. He tries to think clearly about the point at which it went wrong. Was it something someone said? Was it something he did? He makes a mental note to try to handle it another way next time.

By facing the truth head on, he can deal with it. He doesn't let uncertainties brood. He takes time for himself to clear his mind. This clearing out process keeps up his self esteem.

He uses a daily planning book called the Helfrecht-Zeitplansystem which allows him to rate his day on a scale of one to five. On a bad day he can look through each of the activities of the day, rating them all. When he comes to a low point, he can see just where it went wrong. The system helps him to link his business success to private satisfaction.

Michael believes in balance in life – not to be a workaholic for the sake of work, but rather to know what your real goal is and to put all aspects of life, business and family into perspective.

He finds his systems of self criticism to be invaluable. 'Through my daily review I can work against "over motivation" and this keeps me realistic and down to earth in my expectations.'

Not bad advice from a top achiever who wants to 'perfect' communication and make great strides in self development. I suspect it's this realistic grip – almost forgiveness of self – that makes him such a well-balanced human being and extraordinary achiever.

ACTION SHEET

Use this sheet, and the action section which follows, to enhance your own sales techniques and achievements.

Ideas for development:
1. *Link buying needs to human needs*
2. *Make the decision the customer's choice*
3. *Take responsibility for accurate communication*
4. *Objections – mentally walk with them, not against them*
5. *Recharge your self esteem*
Others as they relate to you are – (complete sheet according to your needs)

- Of the above ideas, which one is likely to yield the best results for you?

- What percentage of sales (or performance) increase could realistically be expected?

- How long would it take:
  to develop the idea?
  to get results?

- Who would have to be involved?

- What date should you start?

- What is the first step you should take?

ACTION SECTION

1 Link buying needs to human needs

The psychologist Abraham Maslow developed a motivation model of human needs which is widely applied to all fields of people management.

'Maslow sought to explain why people are driven by particular needs at particular times,' says Philip Kotler[3] in his classic work, *The Principles of Marketing*.

'A person will try to satisfy the most important need first . . . then the next important need.'

Michael Renz does a thorough needs analysis, links needs to the pyramid in the order of the prospect's priority, then presents benefits to meet those needs – *preferably ones no one else can offer*.

One big advantage I see in this is that you can group the features and benefits of your product or service into the five layers of the pyramid. These groupings help your mind to remember them all. Then, when you've identified which layer the prospect's needs fall into, your mind can concentrate on that grouping of benefits. Choose the one that best fits and don't be distracted by the thousand and one other things that your mind is occupied with.

In other words, it's a filing system of benefits for the mind.

Think about your own features and benefits. Choose a layer for each of them in the pyramid. This will put order into your presentation. It will help you make sure the presentation meets the prospect's needs, and increase your closing rate.

2 Make the decision the customer's choice

'People must have strong points of argument in order to make up their *own* minds,' says Michael.

As salespeople, it's often easy for us to see the solution to a prospect's problem. But the sale doesn't come until *they* see it. Because you have more experience with your product and service than the prospect does, it's all too easy to presume they see it as clearly as you do. Then sales are lost because the prospect's *own* mind hasn't grasped it.

Michael doesn't fall into that trap. He realizes that he has to spend as much time as is necessary with the prospect, asking the right questions and giving the right arguments. Throughout it all he makes sure he has covered the four classic phases of selling – the warm-up, the customer needs analysis, the presentation (to meet the needs) and the closing. Then the closing is easy.

When he's sure they've had enough arguments to make their minds up, he closes – 'Let's fix these points we spoke about.'

[3]Prentice Hall 1986, p. 179

Are you starting the close before giving customers enough 'strong points of argument' to make their *own* minds up? If so, refer back to 1 and strengthen your skills in grouping your benefits according to the needs pyramid. That way you'll have an inexhaustible list of benefits in each category to draw upon.

3 Take responsibility for accurate communication

'If I hear you correctly' and 'Let's review what we've agreed.' Are these phrases you use throughout your presentation (or in management meetings)? If so, you're probably well advanced in your communication.

If not, you may want to reflect on Michael's style. When he communicates, his mind is not firstly concerned with what his answer should be. His first concern is, 'Do I understand the other person completely?' The benefit of this is threefold:

- It sets a relaxed environment in which the customer feels cared about.
- It focuses your mind and makes you come across as having a helpful problem-solver style, rather than a hard-sell style.
- Your mind, in this relaxed state, can come up with the right benefits to present, while you are probing to clarify the needs.

Is your first priority in any meeting: 'Do I understand the other person completely?' Why not try it? I promise you that your results will not only increase your sales and your management skills – they will also be 'life changing'!

4 Objections – mentally walk with it, not against it

In *Your Pursuit of Profit*, Bill Sykes and I put forward a three-part formula for overcoming objections: the sympathy segment, the explanation, the satisfaction segment.

Renz handles the sympathy segment with the most ease and finesse of anyone I've seen. By the time he's finished mentally walking *with* the prospect, taking him further *in the direction* of his concern, taking him even *deeper* into the objection, the prospect is so thoroughly convinced that Renz understands that he is ready to hear the explanation.

Renz stays with his sympathy as long as necessary. If the prospect has three versions of the same complaint – the image of the competitive car is newer, it's 'in', the design is better – he may use one or all three of these points to probe further.

How do you handle objections? If you take steps to walk in the direction of the objection to validate it, the prospect will hear your explanation. Your closing rate will improve dramatically. What can you do to be more proficient?

5 Recharge your self esteem

Of all the high achievers I talked to, Michael Renz was the only one who discussed how he deals with his own mind, and the feedback – positive or negative – he gives himself.

It would be interesting to know how the others handle it, and to what degree that feedback contributes to their success. We know for certain that *what the mind tells itself is far more important than actual events or opinions of others to our self esteem and to our feeling that 'we can do it'.*

Michael realizes that, too. He does a clearout when things go bad. He finds the exact point where he went wrong. This helps him decide what to do about it and stops unnecessary brooding.

Some experts suggest taking it further. Even the preacher, Norman Vincent Peale[4], advises 'mind-emptying' exercises. In his bestselling book, *The Power of Positive Thinking*, he says, 'I recommend a mind-emptying exercise at least twice a day, more often if necessary. Practice emptying fears, hates, insecurities, regrets and guilt feelings.' He calls this a mental catharsis.

Then, you might ask, what do you replace these thoughts with? Michael thinks of the personal qualities to overcome the rejections faced in the sales process.

What about you? What are your qualities? In my motivation seminars I have participants give each other feedback on qualities they see in each other which will help them reach their goals. One man, as a result of the exercise, called me the next day to say he had tackled a longstanding issue with his boss which had been lingering for two years in his mind. 'I'm 80 per cent there,' he said, 'because I realized I had the qualities to handle it. I just never realized I could apply them to this situation.'

By handling it, his self esteem was up. Even the thought of *being able* to handle it made him euphoric. By letting it brood for two years his self esteem had gone down.

To keep self esteem up, we have to tackle each issue as it comes up. Michael has a walk in the woods. No matter how busy he is, or how tired, he clears it out that night.

What do you do? Why not turn over a new leaf? Do a mental catharsis to get rid of the junk – the negative untruths – identify the truth so you can do something about it, then think of your qualities and how you can apply them to solve problems and handle new situations.

[4]Cedar/William Heinemann 1988

CHAPTER SIX

Efficiency, Fun and Profit on the Telephone

"Even awkward customers are likeable"

JON BICHENER
Travel Industry US/UK
USAirtours

It wasn't until I took sales training that I realized that EVERYTHING IN LIFE IS SELLING.

'What's the biggest thrill you get in sales?' I asked Jon.

'It's when I had a sale so big that I couldn't fit the numbers on my computer screen!' He recalls the first time it happened, when a party of eight booked a Caribbean Cruise and travelled across the Atlantic by Concorde. 'I loved seeing the numbers come up on the screen.'

For a guy who's never had a sales job before, Jon isn't doing badly.

'I never thought of myself as hard enough to sell. Somehow when I thought of selling, I thought of double glazing.'

In 1948 fate changed his life. An old school friend needed help turning his travel company around after buying out his partner. Jon came on board and, together with a third old school friend, they took the company from a £20,000 debt to profit in three months.

'Then I discovered you could sell without doing something you abhor,' says Jon. The team of three took sales to one million the first year, one and a half million the second, three and a half million the third.

Their sales per employee the first year were worth £427,900 as compared with an industry average of £106,600 per employee!

Yet they don't spare service in their aggressive salesmanship. They have one of the lowest customer complaint ratings in the industry.

Now in their fourth year, they've grown from three to 20 employees, and Jon is selling his way to the start of a new division which he hopes will gross a half million in the first year.

The bulk of Jon's business consists of people who want a ticket fast, that's reliable or cheap.

Since USAirtours are leaders in the industry in sales per employee, this means Jon has some fast talking to do while still keeping customers happy.

DEVELOP A SHORT, FRIENDLY, EFFICIENT TECHNIQUE

'There is a fine balance between minimizing the time spent on each call, and being friendly.' And he must keep the balance to stay at the top. How does he do it? What are the secrets of moving through 200 incoming calls per day, while being absolutely accurate and keeping customers happy?

'The hardest thing I found in the beginning was dealing with *awkward customers*, such as people who talk on and on. Now I've learned several techniques for dealing with them, and this really cuts my time down. We used to take calls 'til 6 p.m., then do another three hours entering the bookings. By cutting my call time, I can now leave at a decent hour.'

Jon remembers the one call that made him determined to find techniques for cutting people short without insulting them. 'One woman, who asked about a ticket to Australia, talked to me for 40 minutes. At first I couldn't get away from her. I kept waiting for her to draw a breath but it didn't seem to happen!

'It went something like this: "My daughter lives in Adelaide . . . She's been there three years . . . It's really interesting . . . They make surfboards . . . When she was here, she was a teacher . . . Now she helps her husband make surfboards . . . His name is Peter . . . He's really nice . . . If you ever go out there, you should meet him . . ." AND SO IT WENT ON!'

Finally Jon interjected with, 'I'd love to. I love surfing. When would you like to come back?'

It was then that he learned his main secret of success on the balance between efficiency and friendliness:

- Always say something to finalize *their point*.
- Then move quickly into *your point* with a question to put them back on stream.

'*Don't* make the mistake,' he warns, 'of using a patronizing style like "Yea, Yea, Yea, that's nice!" You really have to say something sincere that links to their interest before you turn the conversation back.'

In Jon's second point, he finds it's important to use a direct question, such as 'When do you want to return?', 'What date are you going?'

'This puts them off their mark! Their immediate reaction is to answer your question and then you're back on stream.'

But you have to balance it with personalized treatment. How do you do it?

TRAIN YOURSELF TO REMEMBER NAMES

Jon thinks name are very important. He learned that on one of the first training courses he went on.

He trains himself to learn customers' names, and can usually remember these and the dates they're travelling in 70 per cent of cases.

'You have to be interested. That's the real key to remembering. I like the people I talk to. And I like travel. That makes a difference.'

He also feels it's important to recognize a customer's voice when you deal in telesales. If he can't recognize a voice immediately, he asks a few questions and usually the name comes into his mind.

Questions such as 'When were you going again?' or 'Where are you going?' usually get the conversation rolling. As soon as he recognizes the voice, he uses the name, 'Right Tom, let's just pull that up on the computer screen.'

What makes the difference between being a success or not as a travel agent?

'You have to have product knowledge and you have to have skill using the phone,' are Jon's two major points. 'And to achieve either of these you have to have interest – interest in your product and interest in your client.'

SEVEN POINTS FOR HANDLING CALL WAITING

With regard to the phone, a key to efficiency is being able to handle waiting calls at the same time as you're finishing off current calls.

'I've seen so many agents go wrong by not being able to handle waiting calls properly,' he says.

What is his definition of properly? Jon has a seven-point guideline for handling the telephone properly.

1. Don't keep either party waiting more than 20 seconds. If this looks likely, he goes back to the 'waiting' person and says, 'This is taking longer than I thought, can I get back to you?'
2. Never go back to the person who's waiting and say, 'What were you saying again?' Always go straight back to your conversation. That's the only way to build credibility and competence.
3. Never keep a call waiting so long that it switches over to another agent or back to the switchboard. Customers get irate being bounced back and forth. Just take their number and call them back if you're overloaded. If someone else takes the call, you may not get the message for a long time, perhaps two to three hours if they're on another floor – and that loses business for you.

4. Perhaps most important for Jon: corporate travel is so competitive that he views *every* call as a chance to lose the business.
5. Keep it fast but friendly. Let your efficiency come through by the pace you use AND keep responding as they talk. Let them know you're there, 'O.K., I've got that, right, etc.' You must say something so they don't think you've gone off to make the coffee!' It's important to show responsiveness, but keep it short. To get through his 200 calls per day, he manages to keep each call down to one and a half to two minutes each. That's quite a feat for booking complicated business and holiday trips! Naturally the initial call takes longer and each client gets several call backs.
6. Use your tone of voice to show friendliness. Always be positive. 'If someone calls me and they sound down, I try to change their attitude. I stay friendly and positive. The best way to do this is to put everything else out of your mind. You can't be thinking about what happened at home and give your customer your full attention. You have to "be there" 100 per cent.'
7. Handle awkward people and complaints by remembering that 99 per cent of the people are nice. If they are nasty, they have a reason. 'I always try to say "I'm terribly sorry, when were you travelling? Let me get the details." I try not to be put off by their attitude. I try to like them. Remember that if they're really fed up and feel hassled, they won't buy again. I try to realize it's up to me to change their attitude.'

There are so many things that can go wrong in the travel industry – hotels, flights, tours – in fact, in any industry it's worth remembering that people often want to be heard out and then to be reassured it won't happen again.

Jon obviously does it right. USAirtours has one of the lowest customer complaint ratings in the industry.

BUILD PRODUCT KNOWLEDGE THROUGH TRAINING

But to reduce customer complaints, the best place to start is avoiding cause for complaint in the first place. And that means accuracy, knowing what you're talking about, finding out if you're not sure. That means product knowledge, product knowledge, product knowledge.

In the travel industry, things are changing all the time. How do you order champagne to be sent to Naples, Florida (and not have it sent to Naples, Italy!)? How do you order tickets for the bullet train in Tokyo? Well, the SABRE computerized system helps with this, but it's an investment.

Jon and his colleagues are forerunners in that as well. Whereas 69 per cent of all American agents have the SABRE system, there are only about 100 work stations in the UK at the moment, although this is rapidly changing. USAirtours have one of the highest investments in capital employed per person in the industry. They believe in technology as an aid to productivity.

And it works. Their gross profit over the last three years was 75.8 per cent compared with the industry average of 17 per cent!

How else does Jon keep up to date. Well, he devotes 10 to 15 minutes a day to trade journals which they pass around the office. He draws upon reference manuals wherever possible. 'You can't know everything – but it's important to know where to find it,' he emphasizes. There are reference manuals for countries, currencies, airlines, airports and consumers. It's endless and essential.

But the most important part of building product knowledge is through training. In fact, Jon can list reasons for training until the cows come home. As we sat talking I detected a special enthusiasm he had for training. And why not?

Four years ago, he had never sold a thing. Now he and his company are industry leaders in sales per employee, profit per employee, capital employed per employee, return on investment and fewer complaints from customers.

Four years ago he knew nothing of the travel industry. So how did it happen? Hard work, yes. Dedication to doing a good job, yes. But, without training, Jon and the company would still be down in the ranks of the average.

What training is best? It aoesn't really matter. Jon stressed that anything and everything makes you better.

'It's not just the course itself. It's the motivation you get as well,' he stresses. 'You work hard all day. At night you collapse. Your mind can't think of ideas. When you go off on even a one-day training course, your mind is relaxed, it's stimulated with new ideas.

'You meet people, too. You get new approaches and important ideas to take back to the office. It rekindles your interest. You come back motivated.'

One of the most stimulating conferences Jon went to was the American Airlines SABRE subscribers' conference held in Nashville. There are over 1,000 attendees, all exchanging ideas on ways they use the system.

'You meet people who have been using the system for years longer than yourself and doing things you didn't even imagine possible. That's almost as important as the actual training from the conferences.'

Isn't it true how we can go away for three or four days, and a whole world opens up to us that didn't exist at home before?

In addition to SABRE, Jon's had diverse training, from British Airways ticketing to Invicta telesales, to customer care courses, to fare calculations, to non-tele sales, to teacher training, to management training to computer training.

He now uses his teacher training skills several hours a week to teach other people in the office how to operate the computers.

As part of his course he learned about personality profiles – the difference between the 'driver and analytical' who are task oriented, and the 'amiable and expressive' who are relationship oriented.

He used this information to adjust his style to be more compatible with both his students at the office and his clients. Jon discovered himself to be expressive. If he's dealing with a driver who's style is more forceful and result oriented, he can adjust to that by coming straight to the point.

This helps him particularly in dealing with customers. One of his main selling points is: 'Find out what you can offer that the competitors can't, then hit them with it.'

HELP CUSTOMERS MAKE UP THEIR MINDS

The problem is that some customers may not know exactly what they want. 'Your job is to help them make a decision without being pushy.'

They might say, for example, 'I've got several points I've got to go through, but I'm not sure in which order I need to do it.'

The answer is not 'Call me back when you know!' This is not the time to throw your hands up in despair. The answer Jon uses is, 'Let me collect some possible routings and call you back.' Then you say, 'I suggest this or this would work well for you,' depending on whether their objective is saving time, saving money, etc.

Sometimes they claim they don't know what they want, but after a few questions their thoughts are clarified. For example, they might say 'I want to go to Australia.' You say: 'Where in Australia?' They say: 'Oh, I don't know.' You say: 'Sydney?' They say: 'Oh no, not Sydney.' You use the process of elimination. You help them make the decision.

Other times you paint a picture. 'Where do you want to go in America? West coast? East coast? Hawaii?' You find out they want a quiet island holiday, away from it all. Then you paint the picture which matches their needs. 'This island is completely cut off. In fact, there is only one flight in a week.' This gives proof that the place meets their needs of being quiet and away from it all.

Or they may want good, reasonable accommodation, but not a hole in the wall. You say, 'This is an excellent motel chain, it won an award in its group (proof), easy to get to Disneyworld from there (added perk). I've stayed there myself (the ultimate endorsement – clients love the personal proof).'

HIS ADVICE TO YOU

For ultimate success in the industry Jon urges, 'Always be ready to learn. Enjoy your work and show it. Everything else will come with training.'

'I try to put myself in my client's shoes and feel as they feel. That makes people easier to understand.'

Good advice to be heeded from a man whose sales figures are more than *four* times the industry average, in a company which leads the field in profit per employee, investment per employee, client retention and lowest complaint level!

ACTION SHEET

Use this sheet, and the action section which follows, to enhance your own sales techniques and achievements.

Ideas for development:
1. *Develop a short, friendly, efficient technique*
2. *Train yourself to remember names*
3. *Seven points for handling 'Call Waiting'*
4. *Build product knowledge through training*
5. *Help customers make up their minds*
Others as they relate to you are — *(complete sheet according to your needs)*

- Of the above ideas, which one is likely to yield the best results for you?

- What percentage of sales (or performance) increase could realistically be expected?

- How long would it take:
  to develop the idea?
  to get results?

- Who would have to be involved?

- What date should you start?

- What is the first step you should take?

ACTION SECTION

1 Develop a short, friendly, efficient technique

In telesales, time on the phone is precious. If you're too long with one sales call, you lose out on others. But if you're too short, you may misunderstand the customer's need or appear to be rude.

Jon uses his tone of voice and speed of talking to imply that time is of the essence. He answers the phone with 'How can I help you?' with a speed that's quick and a tone that's helpful.

He never goes off the point for long and he has a technique for pulling people back to the point. He says something to finalize their point, then quickly asks a question to pull them back to the issue.

What can you do to make your calls shorter without losing the friendliness? Think of your tone of voice, the speed you speak, your skill in using questions to bring customers back to the point.

2 Train yourself to remember names

Dale Carnegie said that a person's name is the most important sound in any language.

Jon uses it to reinforce his friendliness while moving at the speed of lightning through his calls. With only one and a half to two minutes per call, he's able to keep a personal relationship going while being efficient.

People appreciate hearing their name from you. Why not use it in every call for a week and see what improvement in results you get?

3 Seven points for handling Call Waiting

It's easy to say that you either have a knack for the phone or you don't. But I remember my own days of telephone selling – it's amazing how people improve with the right guidelines.

Jon has seven call waiting points. He says that mastering these can make the difference between success and failure.

Which ones can you improve? Do you keep either party waiting more than 20 seconds? Do you forget the thread of conversation when switching between them? Do you let calls switch over to another agent or back to the switchboard?

Jon views every call as a chance to close business. Good point. Do you and your people see it that way?

Are you fast but friendly? Do you use your tone of voice for maximum efficiency? Do you handle awkward customers and complaints with the right attitude?

If you only had one of the seven points to change, which one would it be? What steps could you take to change it? What results could you expect?

4 Build product knowledge through training

The first thing I have to say about training is that you have to get people's support for it. You'll read more about this in Chapter Ten, in the section *get support for change by asking questions.*

I remember the first sales skill training I ever had. There was a group of ten of us and we had a one and a half hour tape-recorded session on getting appointments. We were to drop our old way of doing things, and, just for that day, try the new technique we had learned in a competition to see who could get the most appointments. The new technique was radically different from the old one we had all been using.

We were set time limits and shown the prizes. There would be a morning prize and an afternoon prize. The gong rang and we all rushed to our desks to start.

By lunchtime I had 12 appointments. The morning prize was given and to my surprise, I won. The next highest was five, and the others had two and three appointments.

'This is strange,' I thought. 'It wasn't a difficult exercise. I just did exactly as the tape recording had advocated. Nothing more, nothing less.'

After lunch I thought, 'I'd better slow down and give the others a chance.' In the meantime I walked around the offices to hear how they were handling it. To my amazement all the others were doing it their old way. They hadn't changed over to the radically new technique although it was simple and straightforward.

At the end of the second half of the competition, even with my 'slow down' technique, the minimum number I could manage to make was eight appointments. The next highest was three.

That made a lasting impression on me which I later took into management, and now into my training programmes. You have to get people's support. They have to be coached along the way. A little adjustment here and a little adjustment there. Then, when the scene is properly set and the learning takes place, the results explode. I got 12 appointments by using the training techniques, whereas the old methods achieved only three to five for the other people.

Jon has built his company results up so that it is the leader in the industry in sales per employee, in profit, in client retention, and in lowest complaints. As we sat talking at the Institute of Directors in London during our second meeting, I asked him to consider everything about his business and tell me what contributed most to its phenomenal growth and success over three and a half years.

His answer came without hesitation. 'Training,' he said. 'Building our product knowledge through training.' He says that his MD spends more on training than any other company he knows in the industry. The results show it.

What can you do to:

1. get people's support of training?
2. provide, and receive more training?

5 Help customers make up their minds

In all industries people often have trouble making up their minds. Sometimes it's due to not knowing the options available. Other times they are weighing up the pros and cons of different options or waiting for more information.

In any case, you can help by filling in more of the puzzle. The more you know about what they need and how they think, the more you can help.

Jon says, 'Your job is to help them make a decision without being pushy.' He gets the ball rolling, 'Let me collect some possible routings and call you back.'

What can you do in your business to help people make up their minds? What questions can you ask? Why not try pulling them closer to their decision each time you speak to them? You'll be doing them a favour. They can then get on with their next problem, knowing this is solved.

CHAPTER SEVEN

The Team Sell

"Together we can shoot down a blind alley and discover new pastures"

THE TEAM, SONY BROADCAST

Broadcasting Equipment
Europe, Africa, Middle East, Eastern bloc

'*The success of team selling is down to the people,*' says Niels Thomas, Principle Sales Engineer.
'*They really have to get along.*' There's no room for in-fighting.

'Who is best salesperson at Sony,' I asked?
'Impossible to say,' was the answer from one of their directors in Tokyo. 'We sell as a team.'
OK, I thought, I'll try again. Perhaps the UK office can identify their top salesperson. I talked to Mitsuru Ohki, at the Sony Broadcast Headquarters in Europe.
'Impossible to say,' was the answer. 'We sell as a team.'
After two in-depth meetings at their headquarters in Basingstoke and four months of communication with Sony in Tokyo, I was won over. They do team sell, and it's impossible to say where one person's responsibility stops and the other's starts.
'It's sometimes hard for people to understand in the West, but in Japan job descriptions are unclear,' Ohki told me.
Why would the Japanese do this? Does it cause chaos? No, just the opposite.

MAKE SUCCESS EVERYONE'S RESPONSIBILITY

'People take on more and more responsibility,' said Ohki. The engineering side and sales work hand in hand, with the attitude of "How much can I do?"'
The result – 'We never have people saying "Oh, this is not my responsibility."'
How does this shared responsibility translate in the West? The Europeans I spoke with at Sony thrive on it. 'The Japanese influence is the best thing that could happen to Britain,' says Niels Thomas, Principal Sales Engineer.

As I sat talking with a team of five around a table, they told me: 'The blur in job descriptions means we have flexibility. We don't feel hemmed in.'

'If we get a bright idea, we can get a team around us and go off on a tangent for a while. The people on the team then feel committed to make it a success,' said John Ive, General Manager of Product Management.

Ive joined the company shortly after it started 11 years ago, heading up the original Research and Development team of four. Now they have 28 in R and D alone, and approximately 450 total people on the 'team' throughout Europe, Africa, the Middle East and Eastern bloc countries.

'Often people think of Sony as being streamlined, but we're not. We're incredibly flexible. Sometimes it doesn't look like we're going in a straight line, and we're not. But sometimes a straight line is not the shortest path to the best result. The diversion brings you something new!' Ive said.

And he meant it. There was something about the way his eyes lit up when he talked about it that told me this was an important part of Sony's success. An important part of the 'ownership' feeling employees get for their success and their responsibility.

With every upside there seems to be a downside. Was there a downside to this feeling of ownership and responsibility?

'Yes . . . STRESS,' John Ive was quick to point out – half joking, half serious – and the others around the table agreed. 'You're bound to worry when you know you're responsible. There's no one to pass the buck to.'

Again the sense of 'ownership' and self direction came back. I got the impression they all felt they were running their own small businesses on every project they undertook.

'But, wait a minute,' I said to Alan Archer, their Senior Manager for Sales Planning, in a conversation later. 'This self direction doesn't go all the way to the top, does it? Surely you have some direction such as sales targets imposed upon you like everyone else.'

'Not really,' Archer insisted. 'Every year we give our expected total sales target to Japan, broken into regions, products, etc.'

DON'T POINT FINGERS – LEARN FROM MISTAKES

'Let's say we project a 19 per cent annual increase. If we don't achieve it, we analyze it and learn from it. The emphasis is on finding out why we didn't achieve it. No one points a finger at you and says, "You didn't achieve your target!" This is unlike any other company I've worked for,' Archer said. And he's worked for one English, one French and two American companies.

'There is no one to point to. We're all part of the team. Naturally the salesman feels bad if we don't reach our targets. But so do the product managers, the project management team and all levels of management. They've all worked hard and wanted the business.'

CREATE TEAM UNITY

Niels Thomas, who closed a £500,000 order on one of the days we spoke, said, 'They've all been part of the picture since the beginning. If I need help, I call in the subject specialist. Product managers are passionate about their product.'

Thomas puts the success of team sales down to three key points:

1. It's essential for members of the team to get along with each other. 'If two of you are in front of the customer and it's obvious that you get along well, that feeling goes across to the customer. It permeates the meeting.'
2. Consolidate your thoughts before a meeting. 'You need to be in agreement on all points in front of the customer.'
3. Have excellent information flow among the team members. 'Everyone needs to know what's been said to the customer on a regular basis. You may be geographically fragmented, but you have to think as a team.'

MAKE IT EASY TO GET SUPPORT

The teamwork is taken for granted as a necessary part of integrating the sales effort. There's no hierarchy to cut through to get support. 'It would be ridiculous to go to their boss. We're all professionals,' says Thomas. He just says to the specialist he needs, 'I'm going to a customer on Tuesday, how about coming along for support?'

Two other people at Sony told me the same thing about teamwork in different ways. 'Let's say someone goes out to visit a customer, and they take advice before they go. If they fail, we can't blame them because we gave them the risk along with the responsibility.'

Ive feels, 'We can't point a finger at anyone else because, if we know more, we should have been involved. None of us are superhuman, neither is the company.'

You get the feeling that it's OK to fail now and again at Sony. It's human nature, it's recognized to be part of the growth and learning cycle.

In fact, when a project is lost, there is a team analysis done of why they lost. It's the salespeople's job to go around to other members of the sales force and factory. They thank them for their efforts and tell them the bad news. So it's important to look at what they do when they analyze failure. It's not a scapegoat analysis. They really want to know – Was it the competition? Did they offer unrealistic prices? Was it the product? Was it something they did which they can learn from and change next time around?

AVOID PRICE WAR

What about price? Salespeople often believe that customers buy on price alone. And sometimes it's true.

Competitors are so keen, in fact, to break into the Sony Broadcast market share, that they offer unrealistic enticement prices.

How do the salespeople cope without getting into a price war?

'I tell the customer to go ahead,' says Thomas. 'As a sales engineer there is nothing else I can do. We have a profit margin to meet.' That doesn't mean they are arrogant about losing business. In fact, it's just the reverse. 'We try never to take business for granted,' says Thomas. 'But, if competitors offer outlandish prices, there's nothing we can do. We still try to woo them back, and often they do come back if the cheaper solution wasn't right. But we don't gloat about it.'

Thomas believes that sales engineers are a breed apart. 'We never try to sell as much as we can. We have to know that the solution is right for the customer.' And they take time to prove it.

MAKE PROFESSIONALISM YOUR KEYNOTE

He remembers one Sony customer who was considering a competitive company. 'He was completely turned off about our product and we were sure he was misinformed.'

Thomas and his colleagues went down and spent the whole day setting up the equipment on the customer's premises so that he could see it operating in his own environment.

And they won the sale. It would have been easy enough to invite the customer up to Sony and save the energy of the set-up. But they didn't. They took the whole day to sell one product, while another could be sold in ten minutes.

Professionalism, being there when you're needed, is what Thomas feels 'keeps our team in first place with the customer'.

Thomas keeps a log of his visits and tries to walk the fine line between seeing a customer 'too often' or ' not enough'.

'How often is too often,' I asked.

'Engineers are busy and don't have time for waffle,' he says. 'But I try to see them whenever I have anything new to tell them. Usually, about once a month.'

And usually there is something new he can talk about – either new equipment, new versions of equipment or new things about the company, such as staff changes which are relevant to the customer's needs.

What makes the Sony team professional? It's an easy word to use, but what do the team members really mean by professional?

'I've actually had customers quote our "professionalism" as the reason we won the contract,' says Thomas. 'Professionalism comes down to your overall image in the marketplace created by the whole team – for us it's:

- maintaining *good* customer relations;
- good back-up on after-sales service; and
- ancillary services such as designing equipment to their needs, or offering training schools to help them operate and maintain their equipment fully.'

NEVER FORGET A SINGLE PROMISE

One-to-one professionalism is also high on Thomas's list. 'Never, ever forget one single thing you've promised to do, no matter how trivial it seems.' He carries a Sony white pocket-size notebook and records everything in it. 'Without this, I'd be lost,' he says.

His promises could include almost anything. 'It could be a silly little thing,' he says. 'I might be talking about something which has nothing to do with Sony – maybe a customer has a problem procuring a certain thing and I know where he can get it. Then I'm happy to get a name or make a contact for him.' This builds loyalty.

He's careful to note it all down, if appropriate, in front of the person. Otherwise he scrambles for the notebook after the meeting.

USE RESPECT INSIDE AND OUTSIDE THE COMPANY

He and the team are also happy to go the extra mile for the customer. 'But not because we hope to win his business,' stresses Thomas. 'This is where the Japanese philosophy of respect comes in. We do it simply because we respect the person for what he is and what he has achieved in life.

'Most of our customers have achieved a level of expertise and we respect them for that. We help wherever we can. We really treat customers as friends, that's what it boils down to.'

Respect, and treating people as friends, is something they do within the team as well. It's something that holds the team together. Thomas quotes the time he was going to talk about an edit system. 'The customer was making a decision about whether our edit system was better for him than our competitors'. I made an appointment to see them and I planned to take along Chris Grey, who is one of our edit systems experts. Suddenly the night before the appointment I got a message saying Chris was held up in Belgium.'

Thomas burnt the midnight oil pouring through manuals in preparation for the meeting which he thought he'd have to handle alone.

'When I arrived at 11 a.m. for the meeting, there was Chris Grey sitting in reception. He had left Belgium at 4 a.m. to be able to meet me, knowing how important he was to the meeting. That's what I call dedication to the team.'

USE EVERYONE'S EXPERTISE

Each member of the team knows they can't be all things to all people. As a sales engineer Thomas tries to call the right experts in for the right customers. 'The longer you're in sales, the less expert you become in any specific product.' With new product developments they have to rely on specific experts.

I wondered if their job became difficult by having too many people stirring the pot, so to speak. I asked him if there is a danger bringing in others who perhaps take a different line and confuse the issue.

'Yes, but we brief people and they respect our guidelines,' he said. They meet at the office or the coffee bar or on the train on the way down. He might say: 'We've taken negotiations to the point that they want a six-machine edit suite. It's probably better not to go into detail on other facilities at this stage.' And so they discuss on which areas to concentrate their sales effort.

Other team members can also influence the sale. One example is their finance expert who made one sale come about through attractive third-party financing, which satisfied the customer's requirements so much that they were able to increase their order.

Employing professionally-minded people is important to Sony's success. The reason they are able to do this, Thomas feels, is because of the personal pride connected with working with a premier product.

There it is. The total package again – the team effort, the quality product, the service back-up, second to none . . . and, of course, the attention to what the customer wants.

DON'T BE COMPLACENT

As we sat around the table, the team remembered fondly their competitive battle to win a multi-million pound system for a major UK company.

The company had been a longtime customer of Sony, but the team wasn't complacent. They knew three competitors were lurking, also wanting the business. The customer was looking for cost-cutting methods of running their operation. Although Sony didn't have an ideal solution at the time, the team went in to look. They reported back to their technical team in London and Tokyo about what the customer needed and collaborated with their US associates.

They started by selling what they had, which was a step in the right direction. It developed an infrastructure. It involved the customer's unions whose members were operators of the equipment.

Then, for a period of one year they developed ideas with the customer. Eighteen months later the system would be ready.

But it wasn't as easy as that. Competitors gave a lot of promises of what they would and could do. The customer flew their engineers over to Japan to study Sony and the competitors. A week's worth of meetings involved part of the Sony UK team, a general manager from Sony Tokyo, a number of Sony engineers from Tokyo, their planning department and, of course, the customer.

The competitors responded in various ways. One flew in a team for hard-hitting negotiation. Another presented a word-processed standard document with an order form attached! Don't forget, this was a multi-million pound system.

USE LOCAL PERSONNEL – ADAPT YOUR WAYS

Sony claims not to be a typical Japanese company. Using locals is an important success method Sony point to.

'We have over 65,000 employees worldwide and only 25,000 are Japanese,' boasts Ohki.

In fact, in the Broadcast division headquartered in the UK there are only 15 Japanese out of some 450 people. In Tokyo they have a good-sized staff of people who speak English. Many staff members from Tokyo have worked abroad. They feel this gives them a cutting edge over the competitors who use translators.

'It's important to learn the language of the country you're dealing with,' insists Ohki, 'because you learn the culture, the mentality and the economy of a country through the language. Without it, you're disadvantaged.'

This particular problem puts more pressure on Sony Broadcast UK than on Sony Japan or Sony US. Because they cover Europe, Africa, the Middle East and Eastern bloc countries, their language, culture, currency and finance problems are multiplied.

THEIR ADVICE TO YOU

What does it take to be a success in sales in this environment?

'You have to be a people person,' says Thomas. 'You have to give people the impression you want to be there, not that you have to be there.'

With 22 years' experience in the business, both technical and sales, he says, *'Sales is the most difficult profession in the world. It's much more difficult than engineering.'*

There is no black and white to selling. 'Sales can be lost because a customer doesn't like a salesman. There's nothing cut and dried about sales. You have to like people.'

Thomas adds, 'It helps to have a sense of humour. All of our customers, without exception, work hard. I try to put a little humour into the beginning of our discussions to relax the atmosphere.'

Most of the sales team are degreed engineers. 'We're not like some companies that use a salesman as an up-front man, then all technical questions have to revert to non-salespeople,' says Archer. 'That doesn't mean that everyone knows everything, though. That's why we rely on the team.'

'We like to feel that we have as much knowledge as the customer and that he can go to any depth of technical discussion that he likes,' says Ive. 'This is important in giving customers the confidence they need to deal with us.'

And again, about the value of the team, Ohki insists, 'None of us can have the full knowledge of all members of our team.'

THEIR STYLE

Sony's style in Broadcast is to sell direct to the major broadcasters. But with 1,400 customers, scattered throughout three continents, Sony sister companies and their dealers carry out the sales function with local personnel.

In addition to being engineering oriented, some have to speak as many as nine languages.

Cultural differences add to the fun and flavour of the sales operation. Salespeople, for example, complete what's called a Major Opportunities Report in each country so that management can revise their sales forecasts. It lists the customer, the project description, the percentage potential of getting the business, and details of order date, delivery request, competition and so on. Some countries are more meticulous than others in their approach to documentation. This all adds to the importance of flexibility and tuning into other cultures.

GOOD COMMUNICATION ESSENTIAL

What else is important? 'Communication is a vital area,' says Chris Whiteley, General Manager for UK and Africa. All of their UK sales team have car phones, for example. Their team consists of a UK sales manager, two senior salespeople, two salespeople and one internal sales position.

'When a call comes in, the internal desk handles it. Typically, people ask price and availability. Our internal salesman tries to find out a bit more about what the customer wants to do. If they ask for the price of a recorder and we ask what camera they are using, we might get a sale for both.'

Then the internal man can pass the lead to the appropriate salespeople immediately through their car phone.

Communication is also important at sales meetings which are held every two weeks. 'We talk around the table about the status of our customers and, if there are any problems or reasons for things happening, our colleagues can help,' says Thomas.

Whiteley points to the openness they use in selling as another reason for success. Anyone can talk to anyone.

Relationships are recognized as important to selling. So, if a salesperson or manager transfers to another location and his customers still want to talk to him, that's OK.

ABOUT PRODUCTS

Products, of course, are another mainstay of the success picture.

'Our products are extremely good,' says Whiteley, 'often exactly what the customer wants without any design modification.' And it's no wonder. With 28 European engineers on board in the UK as an extended arm of the research and development team in Japan, a substantial proportion of time is spent on product development.

'Our engineers don't sit in a corner and design a product, then pass it to the sales department to sell, like some companies,' says Archer. Salespeople, research and development people, and the product management people visit customers on a regular basis. They learn to live and breathe what the customer needs.'

Ive spends 20 to 30 per cent of his time in customer meetings and another 20 per cent with salespeople.

Then there is the time spent 'selling ideas' to Japan. When they've decided on what the customer wants, they need the support of Japan to produce it.

Will the product sell in other countries? Is it moving in the direction we want to go? Will it be strategic to sell it?

WHY DO THEY STAY?

What makes people like working for Sony and stay motivated? John Ive, for example, had two previous jobs, one for two years, one for four years, and now Sony for 11. He's been there since the division started. And judging from his enthusiasm as he talked with me well past quitting time, I would guess he'll be there for a long time to come.

As to what the team members like most about working for Sony, the answer from most was, 'I like the degree of freedom we have. We shoot off down a blind alley for a while and see where it takes us.'

Ive has taken an interest in management styles and what makes a good marketing company. 'In Japan, the attitude is that if someone has a good idea, you allow a group to form and to pursue it.' This obviously allows freedom.

Ive also likes 'the opportunity for changes'. Another perk for him is dealing with other people in the company on a very senior level – building a colleague base in Tokyo. He enjoys being invited to Japanese homes for dinner – it all adds to the excitement, the collaboration and the teamwork.

Alan Archer likes it, because its down-to-earth, informal. 'Personal relationships make working easier. We don't send memos, we just walk into people's offices or call an informal meeting.'

'And the Japanese have a way of putting people at ease,' says Thomas, 'that makes working life more rewarding.' He fondly remembers a customer meeting he had early in his Sony sales career. One of the senior Japanese managers came and sat down next to him to ask how he was doing. 'He made it clear to me that he knew I recently joined. That personal touch means a lot,' said Thomas.

There also seems to be a feeling of acceptance of each other as an integral part of the team.

He recalls thanking one of the Japanese product managers for demonstrating the equipment and how grateful the manager was to be acknowledged. 'I could have just taken him for granted, after all he was "just doing his job". But I didn't. I like the way the Japanese are so respectful of another's place on earth,' says Thomas.

ACTION SHEET

Use this sheet, and the action section which follows, to enhance your own sales techniques and achievements.

Ideas for development:
1. *Make success everyone's responsibility*
2. *Don't point fingers – learn from mistakes*
3. *Make it easy to get support*
4. *Use respect inside and outside the company*
5. *Use everyone's expertise*
6. *Don't be complacent*
7. *Good communication essential*
Others as they relate to you are – (complete sheet according to your needs)

- Of the above ideas, which one is likely to yield the best results for you?

- What percentage of sales (or performance) increase could realistically be expected?

- How long would it take:
  to develop the idea?
  to get results?

- Who would have to be involved?

- What date should you start?

- What is the first step you should take?

ACTION SECTION

1 Make success everyone's responsibility

When people take ownership of an idea, they also take responsibility. 'If we have a bright idea, we can get a team around us and go off on a tangent for a while. The people then feel committed to make it a success,' says Sony's General Manager for Product Management.

The truth is that people don't feel responsibility for something which is not their own. Sony has job descriptions with unclear lines of demarcation. 'We never have people saying "Oh, this is not my responsibility."'

If you want to have success in team selling, you have to create this joint feeling of responsibility. You can't do it with everyone off doing their own thing, doing their job only, leaving the rest for someone else. This leaves gaps. It leaves grey areas which no one picks up.

In short, you have to develop a new culture in your company. You'll need continually to reinforce a blur in job descriptions. You'll have to create an open-door policy between everyone – employees and managers and directors alike. It won't be easy – but it may be worth it.

What steps can you take to make success everyone's responsibility?

2 Don't point fingers – learn from mistakes

To fail is human. But you wouldn't know it in some companies. At Sony, failure is looked upon as an opportunity to learn, an opportunity to avoid the same mistake next time.

Failure is a part of human growth. When children learn to walk, we don't scold them every time they fall down. If we did, they wouldn't try again. Instead we encourage them. We cheer every time they succeed.

Are you pointing fingers? Or are you learning and cheering? What steps can you take to put emphasis on learning and take emphasis off failing?

3 Make it easy to get support

'It would be ridiculous to go to their boss,' says Principle Sales Engineer Thomas. 'We're all professionals.'

Yet I know companies in which talk between sales and service and technical personnel is discouraged or prohibited. No one learns from the other. There is disharmony between departments. Sony knows better. They make it easy to get support. They cut the red tape.

Sure it means there are distractions. It means people have less time to do their 'own' job. But the point is that 'everyone's job is to sell'. That's what the 'team' stands for.

What steps can you take to make it *easy* for salespeople to get support? What result would you expect? Would it be worth it?

4 Use respect inside and outside the company

Niels Thomas called me one day and wanted to move our appointment forward by a couple of hours. He was very apologetic for wanting to change it and made it clear that, if it was not convenient for me, we would leave it as scheduled.

Later when we met he explained, 'We have great respect for you as a person and what you've achieved as a professional, Christine. I wouldn't want you to think otherwise because I had to try to change the appointment.'

It was a nice touch to be on the receiving end of respect. By verbalizing it he reinforced it.

'We go the extra mile for people simply because we respect them for what they are,' says Thomas. And this goes for colleagues and customers alike.

He practises what he preaches. He feels it through and through. He uses it in every aspect of his business and he feels the results from it – undoubtedly respect for himself as well as his fellow man.

What benefits could you derive from adopting a stronger feeling of respect, inside and outside your company?

5 Use everyone's expertise

As Thomas and I sat in the Sony cafeteria reviewing the finished manuscript, each with a cup of hot chocolate on a blustery day, he reflected on what really makes a team 'work' or 'not work'.

He's been part of both. Sony definitely 'works'. 'It's down to the people,' he said. 'They really have to use people's expertise. There's no room for in-fighting.'

Simple and straight to the point. '*There's no room for in-fighting.*' In a real team environment there is positive energy created by collaboration rather than negative energy which goes into in-fighting. We may not agree with another person, but in a team the atmosphere can be some open discussion and respect for another's point of view.

The best course I've seen for opening people up to others' points of view which can lead to healthy collaboration is one called 'Life Training', run by the Kairos Foundation.[5] It's run in both London and the US, and can do more to open people's minds up in two days than people can normally do for themselves in a lifetime.

At Sony, where there is less finger-pointing than most when something goes wrong, and where there is respect for people inside and outside the company, the scene is set for collaboration. Thomas feels free to use everyone's expertise and he calls on the right person for the customer or situation in hand.

[5]Life Training Centre, Kairos Foundation, 16 Talbot Road, London W2.

What can you do to lessen the in-fighting and heighten the collaboration? What can you do to set the scene for unhampered participation by all so that everyone's own particular expertise can be drawn on to the fullest?

6 Don't be complacent

The Sony team know that they have a well-respected product with excellent service back-up, but they don't rest on their laurels. They pull out all the stops each time to prove what they can offer to the customer.

Yet I'm always amazed at companies which bid projects without the necessary sales effort and support. Whether it's that they don't have the necessary know-how or manpower is immaterial. Regardless of how good their product is, their reputation can be destroyed by being complacent about sales – by giving customers the 'feeling' they don't care if they buy or not.

Do you ever show signs of complacency in your bid, in your presentation, in your follow-up? If so, what steps can you take to eliminate them?

7 Good communication essential

Niels Thomas says earlier in the Chapter that 'Everyone needs to know what's been said to the customer on a regular basis'.

He stresses the importance of consolidating your thoughts before a meeting so that you can be in agreement on all points in front of the customer.

Chris Whiteley makes sure his team has car phones. He talks about the importance of openness between employees and with customers.

Communicate, communicate, communicate. Michael Renz (Chapter 5) says that, even with the most open communication, he believes there are errors in understanding some part of the communication process at least 50 per cent of the time. That's with good open communication. What chance do we have with restricted communication?

Why not take a leaf from Sony's book and make good communication essential? What steps can you take, between employees and between yourself and the customer, to improve communication?

CHAPTER EIGHT

Door to Door with Pride

"When you're enthusiastic, the customer is too"

OVE SJÖGREN
Sweden
Vacuum Cleaner Sales, Electrolux

'The hardest part of door-to-door sales is getting in the door,' says Ove Sjögren, the legendary number one sales person in Electrolux for 16 years.

With no previous selling experience, he sold 28 vacuum cleaners in his first two weeks, and 65 by the end of the first month.

Before he started, the sales team used to applaud anyone who made three sales a day. Ove did that his first day on the job. Then he went on to set his own personal record of 11 sales in a day.

After only five years in the business, he had sold more vacuum cleaners than anyone else in the world in their entire career. Now he averages an astounding 800 to 900 per year which breaks down to four or five a day while he's on the job.

With a room full of trophies, albums full of press clippings and memories of accolades galore, Ove is modest about his success. 'Anyone can do the same thing,' he says. 'They just have to use persistence, be willing to be the best and have energy.' But, his colleagues who try to emulate him doubt that it's that easy.

Ove thinks that 80 per cent of people are in the wrong job and many could be a success in sales if they just tried it. 'But you have to get over the stigma connected with sales,' he feels.

When he left his £5,000-a-year painting job in 1972 to take up selling, his friends thought he was crazy. By the end of the first year at Electrolux he was earning £30,000.

Since then he has multiplied that figure, but it's not just the money that counts. It's the satisfaction of helping people. 'When I come back to see how people like their machine and find them enthusiastic, I get tremendous satisfaction,' says Ove who feels that his clients are his friends.

STIGMA OF SALES? OVERCOME IT WITH BELIEF IN YOUR PRODUCT

The advice he gives people to help get over the stigma of sales is to 'believe in your product'. For him it's important that Electrolux has built a reputation since 1912 for giving customers the best possible product. He can sell with pride because he can prove its quality. 'If you buy another vacuum in a shop, you don't know what you're getting,' he says. 'We can prove ours is the best.'

It helps also to put your product in the right perspective, he advises. 'Nobody likes cleaning,' he says. 'I can give them a product which saves them time and gives them a better result.' That's worthwhile.

His philosophy has paid rich dividends. He now has 12,000 customers who he feels are friends. He achieves two top performer trips a year sponsored by Electrolux – 'the Gold Medal' award for the top Swedish salespeople and 'the Gun' for the top five in the world – and he enjoys eight weeks holiday with his wife per year, five from the company, plus three extra he takes himself.

Not bad after being a painter for 13 years. As I talked with Ove, the question I kept coming back to was 'How did you do it?' How does a person go from being a painter with no sales experience to being the best in a world-renowned company – and stay there every year for 16 years?

Is it natural talent alone? Is it drive? Is it technique?

Is it a combination of all three, and if so, what proportion of each?

After a day and a half of in-depth discussions, we agreed that it was indeed a combination of all of them. Ove contends that anyone can achieve the same, and I can agree with that, providing people develop their *natural talent and drive* early in life as well as they develop *technique* later in life.

DEVISE YOUR OWN SYSTEM

Ove seems to have an uncanny talent for systems. As a painter, he watched how everyone else did it. Then he devised a system.

His system, according to his colleagues, allowed him to 'destroy the piece work rate'. When other people climbed up and down ladders, Ove set up scaffolding. When other people washed brushes in the morning, he did it the night before. When others got by with old, inefficient equipment, he bought new.

It took him longer in the beginning to set up the scaffolding, but it saved him countless hours overall. By doing the brushes the night before, he could use his valuable time and energy on the project where it counted in the morning. By investing in the latest equipment, he improved his productivity.

The system involved planning. It wasn't just overall planning, it also involved day-to-day, step-by-step, planning. 'I always knew *exactly* where I was going to start the next day,' he says, showing that the step-by-step plan was always in his mind. 'My colleagues said they could set their watches by my schedule.'

When he decided to try selling for Electrolux, he used the same systems approach. He went out for a day and watched another salesman. Immediately he saw ways of improving the system. 'I work at a faster pace,' he thought. 'I can definitely make the product more interesting, and I can work with fewer coffee breaks.'

BELIEVE IN YOURSELF

'Hum,' he thought, 'if this man is earning a reasonable living, I should be able to do infinitely better.'

So, after one day on the road observing, he decided to give selling a try for two weeks. He was on leave from painting, recuperating from hospitalization, so he had two weeks to spare.

On his third day on the job he had a lucky break. A district manager from Electrolux, one of three heading up the Swedish sales force, came to do a training demonstration.

'His system was like the one I wanted to use,' said Ove. 'This fired up my enthusiasm. The district manager had a fast pace and was interesting to listen to – he made the product come alive.' At that moment Ove had an overwhelming feeling that the job would 'fit me like a glove'.

He called his painting boss, who had been a long-time colleague and friend, to tell him he had decided to sell vacuum cleaners. 'He collapsed laughing,' recalls Ove. Then he had his wife to convince and his parents who he was sure wouldn't approve of the door-to-door sales image for him. It was a tough inner battle, but he had his quality of determination to draw on which, he says, every successful person must have.

DEVELOP A SUPPORT BASE

His wife, although sceptical, was soon won over. 'In fact, I put 50 per cent of my success down to my relationship with her,' he told me. He has a car phone and they talk three or four times a day together. 'It's great moral support to have someone to talk to when you're selling door-to-door. We talk about how I'm doing and we set goals together.' She combines her career as housewife with supporting his activities – accepting shipments, storing inventory and so on.

Then when the day is finished, he calls her, and they have dinner at home together to discuss the successes of the day.

But it's not all work. Next month they will go to Majorca, the following month to Thailand, and the following month Ove will be off to Monaco for the Electrolux Gold Medal Award.

HAVE HIGH DAILY TARGETS

On a good day his work finishes at 4.00 p.m. On other days he works until nine or ten in the evening. He's not a workaholic for the sake of it. He sticks to his targets and when they're achieved, he quits.

The difference between Ove and most salespeople is that his targets are high. At the company they stopped applauding anyone who sold only three machines in a day. Ove loads up five machines a day into his Volvo and expects to sell all of them. 'When the car is empty, I stop,' he says. When it's not empty he keeps going.

Earlier I said that I agree with Ove that anyone can have this degree of success. My proviso was that they should learn to have drive, or determination as Ove calls it, *early in life*. For Ove, his grandfather was a great influence. 'He taught me how to ski as soon as I could walk,' he said, 'and by five he was timing me for ski racing.'

At eight, Ove heard there was going to be a ski competition between all schools in the district and he decided he wanted to win. He practised a lot, in fact, 'every spare minute.' His main interest was sports at that age. He read about top sportsmen and set the goal to be the best.

There were 120 people in the ski competition – all people who grew up with snow, who skied to school, who practised like he did. It wasn't an easy victory. He took the prize which set the scene for the rest of his life. 'With energy, determination and willingness you can get to the top,' he says again and again.

As a teenager it was 'bandy', a Nordic ice hockey type sport, and later it was table tennis in the National Service where he applied his determination to win and took the regiment knock-out prize. All proving that if vision to win, and determination to work for winning, comes early in life, it sticks long and hard.

Another important part of the success formula is technique. Even for those who have less talent and drive – for those who didn't have grandparents who ingrained competitive spirit – technique can go a long way.

Ove has improved his own technique over the years. He used to have to knock on 40 doors to get demonstrations. Now he knocks on 20, gets eight demonstrations and sells to five.

DEVELOP SYSTEMS TO BREAK THROUGH THE HURDLES

He breaks the whole thing down systematically into three hurdles that he must get through:

1. Getting past the door.
2. Getting into the demonstration.
3. Getting over the price objection.

He's set up definite rules for himself to help him get over each hurdle and onto the next stage.

GETTING PAST THE DOOR

'First impressions count the most,' says Ove Sjögren. 'In fact, the first 20 seconds are the most important.' Everything from the way you ring the doorbell to the way you look counts.

He sets a structure in his mind for each phase. 'Two short rings of the *door bell* sound friendlier than one long ring,' he says. And so he gives it two short rings.

'When they open the door, they see more than just you. They *see what's behind you, too.* It must make the right professional impression.' So he washes his car every night and parks in front of the house to frame the picture with the right impression.

'They must first take you in at *a distance that won't frighten them*, but you have to move up to start direct contact,' he says. So he stands well back from the door and off to the side where they'll see him upon opening the door. Then he pauses a moment, and moves forward to shake their hand.

'You must *look absolutely professional* to gain their trust, or you won't get in.' And, if you don't get in, you don't sell. So he advocates a tidy shirt-and-tie business look. Nothing should be forgotten – clean collar, clean-shaven, immaculate hygiene – body odour and dirty fingernails won't do. 'Anything that detracts from your professionalism will ruin your first 20 seconds.

'They must instantly *associate you with a reputable organization*,' he says. And so he holds his Electrolux black leather binder up where they can see it. The company name shows as well as his company ID card with his photo.

'You must *come across unobtrusive, but friendly*, at the same time.' And so after they open the door and take him in visually, he steps forward and says, 'Excuse me for calling'.

'*Names* are important to people.' So if there's a name plate on the door, he'll say 'Are you Mrs Andersson?' Then he follows with, 'My name is Sjögren and I'm from Elextrolux.'

And last, but not least of the 20-second first impression, is the *hand shake*. 'You have to make direct contact with the customer,' he says. 'If the customer doesn't shake your hand, you won't get that necessary direct contact.' He always pursues because he thinks sales fail 99 times out of 100 without that personal contact handshake and the trust that results from it.

Then he leaps right into the *question*. 'Do you mind if I come in for a moment?' If the 20-second trust has been successful, he gets in.

If not, he gets a 'No'.

That doesn't deter him. He continues with the same line of

questioning as he would if he got in. 'You have Electrolux equipment, I understand.' (He doesn't know, but it gives them a chance to correct him.)

Whether it's Electrolux or not, he asks, 'What model?' If still on the doorstep and they're not sure, he asks, 'Can we take a look?'

At his initial question, 'Do you mind if I come in for a moment?', with the right trust built up, 15 out of 20 people will have already let him in. After a few more questions ending with 'Can we take a look?', three more will let him in. All in all, after two minutes he has perfected the technique of being accepted past the door in 18 out of 20 households.

GETTING INTO THE DEMONSTRATION

All the while, his aim is to get into the demonstration.

They say, 'We're happy with the model we have.' And he says, 'What do you want improved?'

They say, 'We think it works fine.' He says, 'Wouldn't it be interesting to see how things have developed?'

Whether they say 'Yes' or 'No', he uses the same positive approach he used on the doorstep – he just continues on with his discussion. He tells the prospect about the differences between what they have and what he's got. With this continuing positive approach he's not rebuffed by a 'No', and sooner or later many people turn their opinion around and become enticed by the product.

He remembers one man who refused to let him in. Upon challenging him, he finally gave in and said, 'You can come in, but I'll never buy.' At the end of the evening the man said, 'I apologize, Mr Sjögren, for my stubbornness earlier. I didn't know about your product and in fact I would like to buy one.' Having so many satisfied customers helps him handle the rebuffs.

By taking the positive approach he is now into the demonstration. He tells them which advantages his machine has over theirs – which, of course, means that his product knowledge is high on his competitors' products as well as his own.

'The hose is conical shaped which means you get more suction and less gets stuck.' This is particularly good for dog- and cat-owners who have problems with hair. If he's selling to doctors, he tells them about the eight per cent fat contained in the bacteria in the dust, or, to any health conscious people, about the microfilter which filters out 99 per cent of the bacteria.

He doesn't see it as selling vacuum cleaners, but rather as cleaning equipment which serves varying needs. 'The side suction can get right up to the wall, or pull dirt from under the couch edge.' If stairs are important, he says, 'You can lay the canister on its' end on each stair and carry it up behind you.' He points out other uses, 'You can use the hot air release option to defrost your refrigerator.'

He also offers any advantage he can to ease people's lives keeping in mind his axiom that people 'hate to clean'. 'If you sign this option with your order, you'll get five bags and a filter through the post every six months and you'll never have to worry about shopping for vacuum bags.'

During it all he's proving the point about how much better his machine works than their old one. 'You can see for yourself how much more efficient it is.' The important thing about the demonstration is that the machine 'speaks for itself', says Ove.

During the sale process he visualizes himself moving step by step, pulling the prospect along in the direction of the contract.

GETTING OVER THE PRICE OBJECTION

Now the customer is suitably impressed by the machine and is starting to wonder what it all costs. They might ask the price, or he might hit the subject head on. Either way his statement is the same. – '*The best thing about this is that anyone can buy this type of cleaning equipment.*'

'There are six ways of paying for it,' he says. This sets the scene and comes before the total price. 'You can pay cash or pay over 12 months, or six months, or two months or 20 days.' But the system he prefers is one that allows the customer to pay a minimum amount upon delivery – about £67 – and then a decreasing amount for 19 months. He likes it because the interest rate is stated separately on each repayment slip and they can pay it off whenever they want. So it's fair for everyone. Ninety-five per cent of his customers buy this way.

Delivery time is short – usually the two minutes it takes him to bring it out of the car.

He never brings the equipment up to the door at the start. He waits until their interest is enticed and then brings in a demonstration model.

GIVE CUSTOMERS HANDS-ON EXPERIENCE

After the contract is signed, he brings a new machine in, fresh in its wrapper, unwraps it and teaches them how to operate it. 'It's important that they have hands-on experience with their *own* machine,' he says. 'It creates pride of ownership.'

Anyone who is at home learns. 'I line them up on the couch to watch. Then they all take their turn.' That includes the husband and the children, too. 'If you're enthusiastic as a salesman, they'll be enthusiastic, too,' he says.

He finds that this enthusiasm and hands-on ownership feeling escalates his sales in two ways:

1. It can teach them to use the product properly. 'If they are tilting the

brush wrong, I can say, "Here, hold it like this and you'll get better suction." ' Therefore the customer satisfaction is increased.
2. Their enthusiasm spreads to all of their friends and relatives.

For Ove this means referral business is up. About five sales per month result from people calling him. He calls this a 'chain reaction'.

Throughout the whole sales process Sjögren uses the 'DABA' approach. 'D' is define what the customer needs. 'A' is get them to acknowledge that they have a need. 'B' is to show that the vacuum cleaner has benefits which meet their need, and 'A' is to get acceptance from the buyer.

Also important to Ove's success is his plan – his 'system'. As in painting he always knows exactly where he'll start each day. He knows every house he needs to go back to if there was no answer the first time. He does that methodically each day at 4.00 p.m. He keeps track of them in a small notebook. He starts on the perimeter of the city and works inwards. More people are at home on the village perimeters and, therefore, the word spreads faster that he is coming. He finds that people start telling each other, 'The Electrolux salesman is in town. He'll probably be over to see you soon.' 'It's an advantage when they expect me,' he says.

ADVICE

As to what advice he would offer other salespeople, he says, 'Work hard. Generate a lot of demonstrations. Be genuinely interested in what you're doing. Don't sound like a broken record. Be original and creative.'

RECOGNIZE THE PEAK BUYING PERIOD

He also warns salespeople to be aware of the 'peak buying period'. He tells of one customer who bought from him and told him that previously they were going to buy from another Electrolux salesman. Just before the order was signed, the salesman asked to use the phone. During his call, they changed their mind.

'When the motivation curve is at the top,' he says, 'you have to act. *You can't get motivation to climb to the peak again.*'

Good hands-on advice from the man who never sold before and went on to break every record in the book.

With these systems Ove Sjögren has set records for the highest number of vaccum cleaners sold in one month – 146 in 1976 and 153 in 1986. Even the ultimate accolade – a diamond lapel pin given for three consecutive years of 330 units a year was crashed – he sold the required 990 units in two years, his second year on the job!

ACTION SHEET

Use this sheet, and the action section which follows, to enhance your own sales techniques and achievements.

Ideas for development:
1. *Stigma of sales? Overcome it with belief in your product*
2. *Have high daily targets*
3. *Getting past the door*
4. *Getting into the demonstration*
5. *Getting over the price objection*
6. *Recognize the peak buying period*
Others as they relate to you are — (complete sheet according to your needs)

- Of the above ideas, which one is likely to yield the best results for you?

- What percentage of sales (or performance) increase could realistically be expected?

- How long would it take:
  to develop the idea?
  to get results?

- Who would have to be involved?

- What date should you start?

- What is the first step you should take?

ACTION SECTION

1 Stigma of sales? Overcome it with belief in your product

Is there a stigma connected with sales? Yes and no. When I was writing this book, I talked to people in every country asking, 'Who is the best salesperson in your industry?' Invariably the answer I got was a famous name of one of their local entrepreneurs who had built an empire. So you see, when people think of the world's greatest successes, they link that success to salesmanship.

When I run seminars I remind people that every building in the world which houses a product or service has a sales function within it. The vast majority are reputable and ethical and we never hear about them. It's unfortunate that the 'used car salesman' image lingers with the thought of selling in many people's minds.

Ove gets over it by having belief in his product and his company. Jerry Gillies says in his book *Money Love* that when you believe in your product and you're enthusiastic about it, it sells itself.

Ove reinforces his belief in his product by going back to people to see how delighted they are with it. He also uses his enthusiasm in the beginning which heightens theirs. He reinforces their enthusiasm after they buy when he teaches them to use their *own* machine, not the demo model.

What steps can you take to heighten your own belief and enthusiasm for the product which will permeate any conversation you have about selling?

2 Have high daily targets

Ove knows what he can do and he knows he can do it consistently on a daily basis. He has a plan and he follows it methodically. He has confidence in his plan and confidence in his ability to follow his plan. He's steady in his determination.

To be top, he has to sell five a day. Therefore he loads five into his car every day. He *intends* to sell them. He doesn't load three, 'hoping' to sell them, and then go back for more. No, he intends to sell five. And he does. He has a positive mind set on five. He has a support base for doing it.

His target is high and he has a competitive spirit for reaching it – daily. Consistency is the keyword. We can't be up one day and down the next. It defeats our morale. Ove is up every day. He made up his mind to achieve high targets and he's done it every day of every year for 16 years.

If you had a solid plan and you followed it methodically every day, could you achieve high targets? Could you be number one? If you could do it, what benefit and satisfaction could you derive? Is the satisfaction enough to motivate you to go out there methodically doing it every day? If not, what is? Find your motivation.

3 Getting past the door

First impressions count. Ove has nine points he observes and carries out to create the right impression in the first 20 seconds.

These are *little* things, all adding up to the *big* picture – the big results. If you're not getting the results in sales you hope for, no matter what industry you sell in, perhaps you're overlooking the little things that really count.

Selling is like a science. If you put two chemicals in a test tube in the right proportions, you get a certain result – the one you were looking for. If you put the wrong proportions in, or you leave out one chemical, you don't get the results.

I remember in 'chem lab' at school, how methodical we had to be in mixing chemicals to get the right result. It's the same in sales. Every *little* thing adds up to the right *big* picture.

Look at Ove's various points from the door bell ring through to the question. How many of these are you doing superbly well?

Great. Now how many need improvement? Can you do them all?

Why not! When you've mastered it, you'll get through 18 out of 20 doors as Ove does.

4 Getting into the demonstration

During the sales process, Ove sees himself moving step by step, pulling the prospect along in a line in the direction of the contract. Each step – getting past the door, getting into the demonstration – is another step closer to the contract.

You notice that his line of questioning is the same whether the prospect answers 'Yes' or 'No' to any of his questions. If he gets a 'No' to 'Wouldn't it be interesting to see how things have developed?', he just keeps telling how interesting things are.

In this respect he's just like Bob Broadley in Chapter 3. Neither of them acknowledges objections. They know their product serves a useful purpose. They get this reaffirmed continually by happy clients and they know eventually this person will change his or her attitude, will buy and become a satisfied client too.

Believe, believe, believe. Your undying belief in the product and in the knowledge and your prospect will eventually be a grateful, satisfied client will get you into the demonstration, provided you continue talking about the benefits you have to offer and not being rebuffed by a 'No'.

Do you give up too soon? If the number one salesman in Electrolux and the number one salesman in National Mutual Insurance succeed by not hearing objections, why not give it a try? Keep your mind focused on your excitement for the product and let your enthusiasm pull you and the prospect along.

5 Getting over the price objection

As Ove and I talked for two days, one of the main points he wanted to stress is how important it is to make the price seem like a *benefit*. Think of it. You can do everything right up to this point. You can get your 20-second impression perfect through diligently practising the nine steps. You can get through the demonstration perfectly with the customer's enthusiasm at an all time high. And then at the moment of truth, you can still lose the sale at the point of giving the price.

Ove turns the price into a benefit. 'The best thing about this is that anyone can afford to buy this type of equipment.'

With this statement he keeps their enthusiasm high. He heightens their anticipation. He quashes their fear that they may not be able to afford it.

Then, with their mind in a positive, open and receptive state, he says there are six ways of paying.

He stresses the payment option which allows them to have the product in their hand now with a minimal payment, and he stresses the fairness of the repayment method. The option is completely theirs.

He makes the price and the payment method a benefit to them. What can you do to state your price as a benefit? Don't reject this idea too quickly. There's always a way to state everything if you find the right angle.

And the results could be phenomenal. What angles can you find to make your price a benefit?

6 Recognize the peak buying period

Remember again that selling is like a science. All the right pieces have to come together at the *right* time. A person's interest is at a peak at a certain moment in time and after that you can't revive it.

In our seminars and in *Your Pursuit of Profit*, we have a long section on the 'peak buying period'. In it we say that trying to revive a customer's interest is like trying to push water uphill with a rake. You just can't do it.

Strike while the iron is not. Recognize the peak buying period of your customer and act then to close the sale. Have your price objection perfectly overcome and close the sale. Close then and only then. Don't wait. Don't kid yourself.

What steps can you take today, to close during the peak buying period? What results would you get? Is it worth the effort?

CHAPTER NINE

Major Projects: Selling with Innovation

"There is no substitute for experience"

DENZIL PLOMER
Europe, UK, Middle East, Japan
Process Control Systems, Honeywell

When Denzil Plomer worked 60 hours a week building electric motors on night shift during the war, he had no idea he'd end up selling multi-million dollar systems for Honeywell over the next 36 years.

Now the most experienced person in Honeywell's industrial division, Denzil Plomer can track his success back to those early days during the war. While posted in Australia with the Fleet Air Arm, he had the opportunity to service the first Honeywell autopilot system, the precursor to those now used on all spaceshuttles.

Since then he's applied his valuable electrical engineering training to projects as complex as space simulation, as big as pipelines across the Assam desert, and as straightforward as refinery pressure switches.

Twice elected to Honeywell's President's Club for top performers, Plomer's philosophy of success is that 'There's no substitute for experience. Selling is a profession in which you never stop learning.'

With such diverse industries to sell to as oil, gas, chemicals, paper and steel, and with such important names as Esso, ICI and BP, it's no wonder that experience counts.

But it's not just the product and the industry you have to understand. Plomer says, 'Getting along with people can make or break your success.'

GET PEOPLE ON YOUR SIDE

More than once in his career his ability to get the trust and support of contractors has allowed him to win major projects against all odds.

He remembers one big project in the Middle East which included Japanese, Arab and American engineers. The General Manager for Honeywell Japan called and thanked him after the project was won saying that they felt that the odds were so stacked against them that they had given the project up as lost the week before.

But it was Plomer's contacts and rapport which had kept him in there. In fact, it was his reputation for getting along with all nationalities that got him there in the first place.

While posted in Saudi Arabia, Plomer had a call from the International Sales Director telling him to go to Japan to help secure the order.

His first step was to ingratiate himself with the contractors. 'I took plenty of time to build a relationship with all sides.' This meant talking with them to make them comfortable with him, entertaining and being helpful on all fronts to build up trust. He had to deal with the Saudi customers as well as the Japanese and American contractors. Having lived in Saudi from 1980 to 1985, and having worked with all nationalities over the year helped him understand the cultures he had to deal with.

Finally, when it was time for the bid, he was the liaison between the Saudi customer and Honeywell Japan who would supply the equipment. They knew the odds were against them as the original specification was written in favour of another supplier.

When the moment of truth came, Plomer had a call from the customer, as is so often the case, saying, 'Your price is too high. It's far more than we want to pay. You've got to reduce it significantly. Come in at 9 a.m. with your "best price".'

HAVE CONFIDENCE IN NEGOTIATING

Plomer knew this was an unrealistic negotiating ploy. 'We've already given you a special price. We can't come down to the price you're expecting,' he said.

He didn't mince words. Continuing, he told them, 'I'm not coming in. We have nothing to talk about.'

The next day the customer called back and said, 'We're calling you in tomorrow at 10 a.m. for your "last price".'

Plomer made a midnight phone call to his Japanese counterparts. Based on their understanding of the competitor, they felt certain that they could win if their price was the same.

But there was more to his strategy. First, he knew that the competitors should submit their price first. With the help of Tokyo traffic, they managed to arrive at 10.20, just as the competitors were walking out.

Secondly, he knew the character of the customer. There were to be four people in the meeting and Plomer instructed that the 'last price' should be in writing in four sealed envelopes addressed individually to each person.

He also informed the interpreter not to let the envelopes be handed out until everyone was in the room. He also specified the order in which the envelopes were to be given out.

'That was the only time in my career when I actually knew the exact *moment* that we won the order,' said Plomer. He took one look at the expression on the customer's face, seeing that the prices were the same, and he knew the order was theirs.

That was a $7 million project which was rumoured two years later to be one of the most successful projects ever done. The project would be worth $14 million today.

The trust that Plomer had developed with the contractors on that project, and in fact over the years in the industry, had helped him to secure the information he needed to win the project.

'It's essential to build a reputation in the industry,' stresses Plomer. 'You never know when or where it will help you.'

BUILD A REPUTATION FOR HAVING THE 'RIGHT' SOLUTION

If you build a track record like Denzil Plomer, it may span the continents as well as the years of your career. The reputation he made for himself back in 1959, working on a 750-mile pipeline project in Northern Assam worth $10 million by today's standards, with 12 pumping stations and 16 booster stations, came back to assist him years later on a bid made in England.

Again, the competitors were seen to have the advantage as they had been recommended by the contractors. But when he stood in front of the semicircle of buyers, there was one man who knew Plomer from the Assam days, and knew he had a reputation for workable solutions.

The man had not been happy about certain aspects of what the competitors were offering and upon seeing Plomer there, he threw him questions left, right and centre. It opened up a whole can of worms, which the buyers had previously not considered, and landed Plomer the instrumentation order for a complete oil refinery with 17 process units!

Much of his reputation comes from looking for *solutions that are right for the customer*. 'Even if it means less money for my company now, giving them the right solution will bring us more business in the future,' says Plomer.

And sometimes this code of ethics even brings immediate results. He remembers one small order worth £35,000 to £40,000, in which Honeywell instruments were specified. In other words, there was no involvement on his part to make the sale, as buying from Honeywell was in the specification.

But during the course of conversation he discovered that the customer had a change of usage of the facility. Consequently, they could get by with a less expensive product.

'I can sell you two pressure switches for the price of one you currently have in your spec,' he told them. You would have thought his order value would be halved. But, not so. The customer was so impressed with the trust built with Plomer that they ordered 300 more units than expected. It opened up a new market for Honeywell. And it built trust with a major customer Honeywell had never sold to before.

Opening up new markets for Honeywell is something he's become known for throughout the company. On one occasion, before the President's Club was started, he was publicly presented with a memento for his accomplishment in securing an order equivalent to $10 million today.

The point Plomer makes is, 'It doesn't matter whether the project is large or small. The satisfaction comes from giving the customer the right solution.'

He remembers one order which he was willing to throw away for the sake of the customer. An experimental laboratory wanted 200 potentiometers to measure hundreds of temperatures, pressures and speeds.

'As soon as I saw the specification I said, "You shouldn't be buying these potentiometers."' Plomer told the customer, 'You should be buying data acquisition systems instead.'

'Since we didn't make those at the time. I was virtually throwing the order away,' he told me.

But the customer was happy with the specification for potentiometers, and Plomer kept in touch with them over the two and a half years of the project development, always pushing the data acquisition alternative although he didn't have one to sell them.

Finally, six months before the final order came due, Honeywell came out with their own data acquisition system, but his problem wasn't solved. They still wanted potentiometers which he thought to be the wrong solution.

LOOK BENEATH THE SPECIFICATION

And this was the start of his long-standing skill of specmanship – the art of getting your solution into the specification.

'I know you must comply with the specification which designates potentiometers,' he told the customer. 'So if you're not going to change the "spec", can you add a rider which says, "If the suppliers wish to offer an alternative solution, they are free to do so."'

When the moment for the bid came, he bid both solutions, while the competitors bid only the potentiometers.

The customer was so impressed with the expansion capability, that they got funding from the Treasury to take it. For very little more, the customer was able to double the capacity of their system.

And, importantly for Plomer, he *again* secured an order for a new division of Honeywell.

The difference between Plomer and the competitors was that they bid 'to spec'. Plomer suggested a better solution, even if it meant losing the business. When he finally could supply it, he added a rider to the specification to accommodate it.

All in the art of specmanship with the customer's needs at heart.

Plomer doesn't let small matters such as not being on the vendor list stop him either.

On one large refining project in Sweden, which he eventually won, he was told by the contractor: 'We're not considering your company for this project, and you're not on the vendor list.'

'Well, I'd like to think we have the opportunity to quote,' countered Plomer.

'That's alright,' was the reply he got, indicating his bid would not be taken seriously.

He went back to the office, feeling dejected, and told his boss about it. Half an hour later the boss was back. 'Here look at this. This will cheer you up,' he told Plomer. It was a new line to be released by Honeywell Japan in a year's time.

'If you can get me a price list and a demonstration unit, I'll get you an order for £100,000,' Plomer said confidently. 'The moment I saw it, I knew it was right for them. I knew I could get the order even though I'd just been told we weren't in the running.'

He got the demonstration unit, tore it apart, and put it back together again. This built up his confidence in the product. He knew it backwards and forwards. This was important because he was the only person in the country who knew the product. He had no one else to rely on. Plomer feels you should always look like you've operated the product all your life when you get in front of a customer.

Now he was ready for the demonstration, but he had another problem. How was he going to get the attention of a contractor who had already told him he wasn't in the running?

PRESENTATION MATTERS – GET THEIR ATTENTION AND KEEP IT

That's when he first developed the idea of submitting a bound quote. This was unique in the industry then, and has now been adopted as standard practice.

The quote included an individually typed sheet relating each aspect of the product to their specification, rather than a glossy brochure, which was standard practice.

He segmented the bid, categorized it, added an executive summary and had it presented in a black binder embossed in gold. He purposely segregated the quote into two sections: one commercial and one technical. This allowed the two departments to evaluate material relevant to them.

That got the customer's attention. And, it got Plomer a demonstration, in spite of the fact that he had the highest bid.

Not bad for not being on the vendor list!

The demonstration was a huge success. But even then the customer's chief engineer was sceptical as it was a Japanese product and never tested here.

PREPARATION LEADS TO CONFIDENCE IN FRONT OF THE CUSTOMER

Now Plomer had a chance to prove his expertise. 'Let's tear it apart and see what it's like,' he suggested. Then they put it together again and it worked like a dream the first time. The chief engineer was impressed.

But a problem still existed – the price. 'We want to go through the bid with you. The only way we can recommend it is by it being the lowest price,' the customer told him.

By working hand in hand with them, through the confidence he'd built in the product, they were able to take the lowest possible interpretation of the bid, remove the enhancements from their product which were desirable, but not necessary, and resubmit the bid.

They won. Eventually even the enhancements were put back in.

The point here was that Plomer knew he had the best solution. But as we all know in today's competitive environment, *better mousetraps don't sell themselves*. Plomer knew he had to get their attention with the quote or they would never get to the demonstration stage. He was told later that all the competitors had supplied 'a few specification sheets which looked tatty by comparison'.

Plomer has always believed that 'presentation matters'. It illustrates a company's professional attitude towards business. He feels that, 'If a customer is placing a large order, he deserves a nicely presented high-quality presentation of the bid.'

He believes in making the bid distinctive. On the Middle East project bid, for example, he suggested to his Japanese counterparts that they put a drawing of the control room in the front of the bid. But he didn't stop there. He specified that the drawing should show operators who looked like Arabs.

And why not. We all relate best to something familiar, rather than something foreign. Would Westerners relate to a project drawing if all the workers looked Arab or Japanese? Probably not.

'Your bid is the window between your company and the customer,' he often tells his colleagues. 'You never know who will look at it. It may be the president of the company. You want yours to be distinctive.'

Because Plomer has built a reputation for getting orders against all odds, he has been asked by management to pass his expertise on to the newer members of the sales force. From the three-day training sessions he has run so far, one man and one woman have been elected to the President's Club. It shows that expertise can be passed on.

When Plomer retires, it won't be without leaving his mark on the industry.

SEEING IS BELIEVING – MAKE YOUR IMPACT

Besides developing a presentation format which is now accepted as standard in the industry, he was also the first to do a full scale mock-up of a control panel. Again his emphasis is on 'seeing is believing'. The more customers see it, visualize using it and understand it, the better your chances.

Before mock-ups had become standard practice, he had to use his ingenuity to overcome an objection. The project had control panels onto which the instruments were to be attached. The panels had been designed around his competitor's instruments which were all six feet high.

As Plomer's instruments were nine feet high, with four horizontal rows, he had to squeeze 12 more inches of instruments per panel into a fixed space. All instruments had to be visible to an operator seated at his station. This at first seemed to be an insurmountable objection to overcome. Plomer thought, 'The only way around this is to build a panel and prove that the instruments can be seen.'

He made several panels, which included 60 full-scale photographs of the instruments, and put a label on each photo just as the tag number would appear on the real instrument. Then he called the customer and said, 'Could we use your office to set up a display?' 'Of course,' was the answer.

Plomer set up his panels with photos attached in the office. He measured the exact distance from the customer's desk to the panel, to ensure it was the same as the operator's station.

The mock-up looked great. The only problem was that the operator's station had an upright back panel which the desk didn't have. *Voilà* – in a streak of creativity Plomer stuck his briefcase up to simulate the back panel. This created the same view restrictions as the operator's station.

The buyer entered and saw the plan was workable. His objection was immediately overcome and the order was taken.

The technique made such an impact that stories still circulate about it. Full scale mock-ups have become part of everyday life.

HIS ADVICE TO YOU

I asked Denzil Plomer what he believed to be the reasons for his success and his outstanding long-term reputation in the industry. 'Being an outgoing person with a cheerful disposition,' was his answer. 'It's important to be dedicated to your profession and never lose enthusiasm despite the ups and downs.'

As to what he advocates for anyone who wants to be a success, he has three points:

1. Integrity – without it you have no standing with customers. If you lose it, you're dead.
2. Listening – unless you hear all that your customers have to tell you, you wont' be able to fulfil their needs.
3. Creativity – plus innovation are the assets which set you apart from your fellow man.

GO *WITH* CULTURAL DIFFERENCES

I noticed as we talked that his approach to everyone in the world was unjudgmental. He takes everyone's differences matter-of-factly and works *with* the differences rather than against them.

Of the Japanese, for example, he says, 'They don't understand negatives so you have to be very careful in wording your questions in order to get an answer which you interpret correctly.'

'Don't you like apples?', for example, could generate a 'Yes'. The 'Yes' means 'Yes, I do not like apples.'

'Use straightforward language, always in the positive form', he advises, 'even in telexes and letters.'

'What if you sent a telex asking, "Is it true this product uses 110 volts?", I asked, thinking I had a straightforward question.'

'That might even be difficult,' he said. 'If the answer was "No", you'd probably get an affirmative answer back such as, "Product suitable for 220 volts."'

'People have to understand each other and be tolerant to have success,' he emphasizes.

Judging from the number of times he's been called to the far corners of the world to liaise on projects, one can surmise that he's used his creativity to develop 'peoplemanship' as well as 'specmanship' to the highest degree.

ACTION SHEET

Use this sheet, and the action section which follows, to enhance your own sales techniques and achievements.

Ideas for development:
1. *Get people on your side*
2. *Build a reputation for having the 'right' solution*
3. *Look beneath the specification*
4. *Presentation matters — get their attention and keep it*
5. *Seeing is believing — make your impact*
Others as they relate to you are — (complete sheet according to your needs)

- Of the above ideas, which one is likely to yield the best results for you?

- What percentage of sales (or performance) increase could realistically be expected?

- How long would it take:
  to develop the idea?
  to get results?

- Who would have to be involved?

- What date should you start?

- What is the first step you should take?

ACTION SECTION

1 Get people on your side

'We had given up the project as lost,' said the General Manager of Denzil Plomer's project, which was not only won but ultimately one of the most successful in the division.

Plomer's success came from getting people on his side. Not just one person, but as many as he could get from all sectors – the customer and the contractors of three nationalities. He made them comfortable with him. He spent weeks building trust with them. Ultimately, he was able to put the pieces of the puzzle together and come out victorious.

What steps can you take to get people on your side? Not just one person, but all sectors.

2 Build a reputation for the 'right' solution

Plomer puts the customer first even if it seems to mean losing business for the company. But the short-term loss proves to be a long-term gain. His reputation for the 'right' solution has followed him through the years and the continents.

'The satisfaction comes from giving the customer the right solution.' This attitude has rebounded and won him business when he least expected it, halfway across the world.

Plomer is unwavering in his determination to provide the 'right' solution. Will this approach help you to win business in the long term even if it means a short-term loss? What steps can you take to prove your expertise in providing the 'right' solutions?

3 Look beneath the specification

Plomer knew he had the best solution. However, that solution was not being called for in the specification. He asked to have a rider put in stating that an 'alternative solution' could be offered. Then he bid two solutions: the one in the spec and his own. He got overwhelming support for his own and he was the only one bidding that innovative solution. Why? Because he was the only one who looked below the surface of the specification to see what the customer really needed.

What can you do to work with your customers to look for their real needs? Remember that their perceived solution might be based on limited knowledge of what's available. You can look beneath the spec to find the best solution.

4 Presentation matters – get their attention and keep it

I remember eight years ago when I started Intrinsic Marketing, one of our first clients was a pharmaceutical company that wanted export assistance. When they gave us their documentation including the technical spec sheets for submission to the ministry abroad, we were shocked. The sheets had been photocopied so many times that they were almost unreadable – certainly unpresentable.

We had them retyped beautifully with bold headings and in a modern typeface. Then we had colour photocopies made of their packaging with the words in their own language. It all looked gorgeous in its presentation folder which preceded the visit. Without making an impact at stage I, there would be no stage II *regardless of how good the product is.*

Don't kid yourself, presentation counts. Don't spend all your time on R and D, on technical discussions, and then ruin your chances with a poor presentation.

'Your bid is the window between your company and the customer,' Plomer says. 'You want yours to be distinctive.'

What are you doing to get the customer's attention with the bid and keep it? If you're not directly responsible for the presentation format, what can you do to implement higher standards? Perhaps people would benefit from reading about Plomer's techniques. Sometimes enlightenment does the trick.

5 Seeing is believing – make your impact

If a picture is worth a thousand words, think what a full-scale mock-up is worth! If you remember that, when people can see themselves using, enjoying and benefiting from your product, they buy. What better way is there than to have a full-scale mock-up so that they can 'feel' themselves in the new environment?

What steps can you take to make a *buying decision impact* by letting them *see it for themselves*?

CHAPTER TEN

The Fast Track

"I'll take persistence through my entire career"

MICHAEL CAMP

Food Industry, Britain Lyons Tetley

I had to wait for my 21st birthday to be promoted in the civil service. So I decided to go to the private sector where I could be promoted.

'His preparation is impressive. When he goes into a customer, no stone has been left unturned in terms of the research and the strategies he has developed,' says Sales Director Bill Durning of Michael Camp, the youngest National Account Manager Lyons Tetley has ever had handle a major grocery multiple.

'He makes countless presentations,' says Durning, 'When one strategy fails, he tries another. He *never* gives up.'

Currently he is Senior National Account Manager at 31, handling Sainsbury – one of the largest and most prestigious grocery chains on one hand – and Kwik Save – known for 'no frills' best price brand names on the other. This requires skill and diversity of strategy which normally take a lifetime to acquire.

But Michael Camp has a track record of developing strategies, of looking for a niche, of breaking down barriers in the industry, which is second to none.

At 21, he took his first junior sales job with Smith's Foods selling crisps, and left his civil service job behind. The rest is history.

When his colleagues were happy to sell one case of crisps, meeting the company target, Camp went back to fill his car with cases four times a day. When his colleagues had a competition to see who could sell to the most customers out of 15 calls a day, Camp raised the stakes and sold to 25 out of 25. 'I always set my own targets,' he says.

That got his picture in the company magazine, and the recognition he wanted for the skill he knew he had.

Still only 21, having been top salesman during his four consecutive months on the job, the company recognized his extraordinary skill and gave him a three-grade promotion to special account salesman. Now he would be selling 3,000 cases at a time instead of three, selling to the cash and carry outlets.

Passing up two grades in promotion did nothing to stunt Camp's growth. He invented his own systems for breaking targets down into workable pieces and servicing his accounts. He was so successful that he was made Field Sales Trainer.

At 23, he was teaching his systems to people who were twice his age and had twice his experience.

Six months later, at 24, he became Smiths' youngest Area Sales Manager, in charge of a team of nine. The team was ranked thirteenth out of 13, and this presented a challenge for Camp. 'I'm going to make them number one in 12 months,' he promised, and he did it in six. They gave him a new team, equally as difficult.

Then at 26, with five years at Smiths and five promotions, he wanted diversity of product exposure, and moved to Spearhead, a food brokerage company. There he was Regional Sales Manager responsible for half of the country with a team of 12 people and 10 different product groups. Instead of one product group, he was learning what made competitors compete and buyers buy in household goods, confectionery, alcohol, beverages and so on.

After 15 months he was promoted to National Account Manager in charge of Tesco. This was his first major multiple with sole responsibility which would stand him in good stead for his entire future. After 12 months with Tesco, they made him one of their three National Accounts Managers in the country in charge of Tesco, Gateway, Asda, Presto, Safeway and Sainsbury – *all the major multiples.*

At 29, with eight years in the industry and seven positions ranging from field sales to sales training to sales management to account management, his entry into Lyons brought a high profile and realistic expectations from management.

'We know we have to keep him moving quickly,' says Sales Director Durning. 'He won't be happy without challenges and we realize that.'

So far Camp hasn't disappointed them. Joining as a Trade Sector Manager of confectionery with a team of six, he brought their new product, 'Cluster', into national prominence in 12 months, breaking into market sectors where they had no previous presence.

And then as Senior National Accounts Manager for Lyons Tetley, he has managed to make enormous inroads with his two majors – Sainsbury and Kwik Save. That's doubling the number of stores for one product, getting another relisted after it had fallen from the list, getting an important product into 180 stores versus the nine it was in, and getting a limited market product into 43 stores versus the ten it was previously in. All in a six-month period!

As I sat talking with Michael I asked him what lessons he's learned that he uses most today. 'I use everything I've ever learned,' he said. 'But of them all, I guess I've learned that persistence is the bottom line.'

USE PERSISTENCE WHEN ALL ELSE FAILS

'When I was at Spearhead,' he said, 'you just couldn't take no for an answer.' His clients counted on him. 'As food brokers we promised our clients we'd get products into stores and we did. Each time was like starting over again. If we failed, we lost our reputation. So we couldn't take no for an answer.'

But when all else failed, he used persistence. He remembers fondly his first sales job and moment in time when persistence paid off. He had two cases of snack food in his arms and when he walked over the threshold of the shop, the shopkeeper shouted 'No'. He went in anyway and sold £6.34 worth of crisps – the greatest sale he'd ever made!

Why? Because, he learned persistence pays off. 'It's the same when selling to anyone,' he says. 'You may have to compromise on the quantity, but if your strategy is right, you should be able to persist and sell.'

His early days in sales also taught him other valuable lessons which he's used throughout his career.

BREAK YOUR OWN TARGETS INTO WEEKLY SEGMENTS

At Smiths when he was given his three-grade promotion to Special Account Salesman, he was given his targets by his manager. Then he developed what he called 'target breakers' for himself.

'I divided my targets into weekly segments on a high/low basis. That meant week 1 was higher than average – I always hit it strong to get started on a strong footing.' Then he had a lower than average target for week 2. This allowed him to spend time in the cash and carry organizing the goods to sell better. He would make sure all the shelves were full, move stock down to eye level and so on. 'If the racks are empty, people don't buy,' he says.

It sounds like common sense, but the fact of the matter is that retailers don't always have time to move products around and refill racks on every product. They rely on reps who should make it their business to restock, but don't always *make* the time. Camp made sure he made the time.

In week 3, he went high again, and in week 4 low, making more time for arranging stock.

Every weekend he spent time developing his targets for the next week, devoting the most time to his highest volume customers. 'It's the old 80–20 rule,' he says. 'Twenty per cent of your customers give you 80 per cent of your business. You should spend the most time with them.'

Where do other people go wrong in sales? 'Ninety-five per cent of salespeople don't break their targets down properly,' says Camp.

For a final touch on targets, he advocates adding ten per cent to the bottom line. He does this both when he's in direct sales himself and when he's managing people.

*1		†2			‡3	
Total Target	Account 101 102 103 104	Target XXX XXX XXX XXX	Week 1	Week 2	Week 3	Week 4
			X high	X low	X high	X low
+10%						
Total						

*1 Add ten% to total target
†2 Break target down by customer
‡3 Break target into weekly segments, high, low, high, low.

HAVE STEPS AND TOOLS

While in that same position he learned the classic rule for selling in the industry which he feels is just as good today as it was then. It can be used on different levels of selling.

It's the rule they refer to as seven times six or seven steps and six tools to selling.

The seven steps refer to planning and preparation, outlet check, stock check, presentation, close, merchandising and administration.

By learning these meticulously he was able to score high marks from his management team when they accompanied him in the field. His overall attention to detail and good procedures was a significant factor in working his way up the ladder fast.

The six tools refer to the planning slip, pen, brand talk, sample, record card and visual aids.

To take an example, let's look at the use of the pen. The pen should be used to point to a specific part of a proposal. It draws the eye to that point. It avoids distraction by such things as dirty fingernails.

But Camp stresses again the importance of attention to detail. 'You must teach people exactly how to use these tools or the exercise is worthless.' If you teach someone to use a pen to point, you must also make them aware that they must pick up the pen and point immediately to the spot. 'Otherwise, they might wave it around while they talk, creating distraction and defeating the whole purpose of the exercise,' he says.

Taking the importance of detail even further he showed me that if he uses a pen as a pointer, he positions it precisely to the right side of the letters or numbers he wants to emphasize. This focuses the prospect's eye where it should be focused.

As I watched Camp explain this, I thought, 'He's absolutely right about detail. There's no point in learning to use something if you don't learn to use it exactly right.'

Sales tools are no different from other tools. If you use an electric saw wrong, you might meet with disaster. You won't get the result you were looking for. If you use sales tools wrong, you don't get the result you were looking for either. Therefore detail matters. Preparation matters. It brings us back to the statement Bill Durning made about Camp: 'His preparation is impressive.'

It brings up the age-old question 'Are good salespeople made or born that way?' Camp taught himself to use the tools meticulously. He *made* himself a number one salesman. He made himself give attention to details.

GET SUPPORT FOR CHANGE BY ASKING QUESTIONS

When Camp became a Field Sales Trainer at 23, he was quickly thrown into the deep end of dealing with people of all ages and types. He had to monitor everyone's performance, then improve it and set objectives for them.

'The first thing to do in working with people is to get their respect,' he advocates. 'Anyone can talk theory. The only way to get their respect is to show them that you can *do* it yourself and teach them a *better* way.

'The second thing to do is *make them see their own problem and their own solutions*,' he says. 'They feel good if they've identified it.'

He feels that most people could become better managers and trainers if they would become practised at open and closed questioning techniques. In trying to get people to see their own problems he asks such questions as, 'What do you think you could improve?'

If they don't know, or if he disagrees, he says, 'Actually, I think such and such, and I'll tell you what, if it would help you, on the next call I'll show you exactly what I mean.' This way he gets their co-operation and support. People only change when *they* want to change.

If the person doesn't identify any areas that need improvement, he uses the direct approach. 'Chris, there are some areas of operation that need to be improved. Let's look at what they are.'

And then he starts the questioning approach again. 'Let's take the point at which you get the samples out. What do you think you could do to improve it?' And so he gets their support for change.

FOUR-PART FORMULA FOR TURNAROUND SUCCESS

Camp's next promotion at 24 to Area Sales Manager probably did more for him in terms of consolidating his skills than any other. In his bid to bring his team up from thirteenth and last position to first, he identified four areas that needed attention. They were:

1. Raising standards.
2. Getting the salespeople to identify when *they* could build volume.
3. Controlling costs.
4. Raising morale.

With this formula, not only was he the youngest area sales manager in the history of the company, but he was the most successful, pulling the team (of the same people) to number one place in six months.

In *raising their standards*, he used the same techniques as he did in training, which we discussed above. He got their support for change by asking questions.

In *getting the salespeople to identify where they could build volume*, he followed a standard procedure for each of his sales meetings. 'First, I would get each salesperson to come to the meeting with their own estimates of how much they could sell to each customer and each product group.'

Before the meeting he would get what he thought to be realistic targets on each. 'Salespeople are overly optimistic,' he says. 'They might sell less than they think they can, but more than you estimate.' So if their own target was higher than the one he set for them with enough allowance for error, he let it ride. 'If you think you can do that, fine. Go out and do it,' he'd tell them.

If their figures were low, he'd say, 'That's not enough'. But he didn't stop there. He didn't leave all the weight on their shoulders to come up with the answers.

He always asked himself, 'What *extra resources* do I have that I can deploy to them to *help them* get higher volume orders?' These resources might be advertising allowances or display allowances – such as an extra fee for putting end rack display in a hot spot, a local mail-shot to customers telling about a special price offering or free stock with volume purchase.

If he didn't have resources to spare, the whole team would look at the shortfall target and decide how to divide it evenly between them. 'If their combined target for nuts, let's say, was 10,000 and we needed to sell 12,000, then we had a 2,000 shortfall. But when we divide this between 200 different calls for each of ten people, it's only one more unit for each call.'

And so the team took responsibility and decision for building their own volume.

With regard to *cost control*, Camp had a fundamental philosophy. – 'You can't give away a free product without a strategy. And the strategy has to prove itself.'

Whereas most of the previous managers had an 'anything goes' attitude about giving away free products to get orders, Camp put guidelines on it. He showed them how to get better results, developing a policy that linked free products to orders. 'If you need to give 100 away to get an initial order of 1,000, that's OK, but don't do it unless you have to,' he told them. It didn't make sense to him that one salesperson would be giving away 1,000 units and another one ten units to get the same size orders.

Costs were cut as each salesperson developed their own strategy, using the free product to maximize their orders.

And last, but not least, Camp *raised morale*. 'People respond well to enthusiasm,' he says. And rightly so. If the manager's not enthusiastic, why should anyone else be?

Once a month the team would meet for drinks or whatever seemed appropriate to build a team identity. 'They need to feel they operate as a team,' he says. 'It's no good when each person is off doing their own thing. The results don't come without team unity.'

WORK CLOSELY WITH YOUR DISTRIBUTORS

Camp's next chance to prove his practices came when he was brought in by Lyons to give their new product, 'Cluster', national prominence. There he had to motivate distributors as he had once motivated his own team.

'The principles are the same,' contends Camp. 'You have to help them develop strategies. You have to employ your resources to help them get your product into the retailer.'

As in all industries the distributors have a thousand lines to sell. Why should they promote yours? The real question is not so much 'Why *should* they?' but 'How *can* they?' Camp realized this, put two reps on specifically to develop it, and worked with the 17 national account managers employed by the distributor to identify the most important customers.

Having identified the major customers within the CTNs – confectionery, tobacco and newsagents – they were able to develop incentive schemes and special promotions to get 'Cluster' in.

If you don't develop a strategy with the distributor, says Camp, 'The customer looks at the "PLOF" – the price list order form – and skips right over new products such as ours.'

In addition to the CTNs, Camp identified three other outlet groups in which they previously hadn't had a presence – petrol stations, chemists and off-licences. Again, with the 80–20 rule, he recognized the majors and spent the most time developing them. 'Within the petrol group, the BPs, Shells and Essos do more than all the rest combined,' he says. The same is true of Victoria, Thresher and so on within the off-licence group.

In working with the distributors he was conscious of getting the price point right. If the only way to get the product in is to allow 10p per case for profit margin or promotion, then he works closely with his own financial team to assess the volume necessary to work at the discounted price.

Then his distributors can go to the customer and say, for example, 'OK, we can improve the margin by 10p per case if the volume goes up by X per cent.'

With this hand-in-hand approach to working with distributors, he was able to bring 'Cluster' into prominence in seven months.

INFLUENCE ALL AND DEVELOP A STRATEGY

Now at Lyons Tetley he's had a chance to draw upon his experience with key accounts, delighting his management with his ability to achieve results in *four* product groups in a few short months.

'Although there are an infinite number of composite elements to getting a marketing strategy right, there are two critical factors,' says Camp. He lists these as:

- The ability to influence the decision of people at all levels of the account. Depending on the structure of the company, these could include people in merchandising, marketing, the person negotiating the overriding terms, as well as the buyer, assistant buyer and so on.
- Developing strategies for what Camp calls 'precision trade marketing' – making branded propositions from your portfolio which precisely fit the customer profile, proving that the customer will gain by them.

His two key accounts, Sainsbury and Kwik Save, have two completely different trading profiles. One of Camp's strengths, remember, is as Durning put it, 'impressive' preparation.

To achieve the inroads with *four* product groups in such a short time, Camp first researched the customer's competitors. After seeing what volume levels the competitors were achieving, he could assess the market potential for his customer. Then he proved his theory as many times and to as many people as were necessary.

To make a visual impact he uses pie charts and line graphs which he gets off the computer himself. He always uses colours to make the concepts quicker and easier to grasp with higher impact.

If he has two similar products in a range, with one retailer stocking both and getting high volume on each, and one retailer stocking only one, he can use the pie charts of the first to prove that selling both *doesn't* mean that the two products cut into each other's market share. In fact, the charts show that having both enhances the sales of both. Naturally it would be indiscreet to say who the customers are, but his charts make the point about volume.

'Once customers respect your judgment,' Camp stresses, 'they'll consider your propositions.' One reason for his thorough research is that he knows that all of his recommendations must be 'spot on'. If he makes recommendations that work and pay off handsomely for retailers, his relationship with them will continue to build, as will the product lines on the shelf.

Another example of matching products from his portfolio with customer needs, is one he derived also from his research. He saw that one of his customers was losing business to a competitor because they failed to sell tea packaged in small quantities. He discovered that the retailer's customers were going down the street to buy that size from other retailers.

The problem was that Camp's company didn't package that size either. However, if he could get his own marketing people excited about the idea and the customer excited, all sides would gain.

First he talked to his own people. 'What volume are we talking about?' they asked. Because he was talking high volumes, they were enthusiastic. With this support, his next step was to go to the customer.

He also had to offer his customer a price that would undercut competitors. This could have been a problem for him if the competitors were also buying this size product from him. But they weren't because that size didn't yet exist. So there would be no conflict of interest for anyone. Everyone would gain.

That's what Camp likes to call 'precision trade marketing'. The supplier gains. The customer gains. The end user gains. Looking for the perfect niche. Creating a win, win, win for all strategy.

PERSONAL LIFE

But looking for the perfect niche is not something new to Michael Camp. He's applied it to his own life with success as well.

At 17 he looked out at the world and saw high unemployment. 'What can I do to create a niche for myself?' he asked. Should he go on to university like his contemporaries or was there a better way? He decided to get some experience first, to give himself an edge over the others with degrees but no experience.

As to why he gravitated towards sales, no one can really say. He comes from an adventurous family with a brother who emigrated to Melbourne, Australia – first with Alcoa then with the National Bank of Australia on the computer side – and a sister who had been in sales in the UK with Rank Xerox.

He gets a lot of support from his family and he thinks that his early upbringing by his parents had a lot of influence on his ability to deal with people. 'The role models your parents give you are essential,' he says. 'Learning when to speak or not to speak, learning not to offend people by what you say, become a basis on which to build.'

Michael Camp's personal life, like most people's, has had its ups and downs – but 'all's well that ends well'. He and his second wife Julie have been happily married for four years and have two bouncing boys, Thomas and Alex.

Despite his astronomical rise in the industry over ten short years, setting new thresholds in nine positions with three companies, Camp is modest when he reflects on his early naiveté in sales. 'I remember my first interview for a sales job when I was 21,' he says. 'It was with Mars. There were 171 people being interviewed and when I got my turn they gave me a chance to ask a question. My question was very profound – something like "Can I use the car at weekends?" ' He didn't get the job, but he made sure he learned fast.

It shows how far one can come in ten short years.

ACTION SHEET

Use this sheet, and the action section which follows, to enhance your own sales techniaues and achievements.

Ideas for development:
1. *Use persistence when all else fails*
2. *Break your own targets into weekly segments*
3. *Get support for change by asking questions*
4. *Four-part formula for turnaround success*
5. *Work closely with your distributors*
6. *Influence all and develop a strategy*
Others as they relate to you are − (*complete sheet according to your needs*)

- Of the above ideas, which one is likely to yield the best results for you?

- What percentage of sales (or performance) increase could realistically be expected?

- How long would it take:
  to develop the idea?
  to get results?

- Who would have to be involved?

- What date should you start?

- What is the first step you should take?

ACTION SECTION

1 Use persistence when all else fails

As we talked in Micahel Camp's office in Greenford, he reflected on everything he had done in his career. 'When all is said and done, it's persistence that counts,' he said. 'I'll take it through my entire career.'

When you think about it, he's right. You can have the best strategy in the world, but if you're not persistent in getting it through, you achieve nothing.

I remember a comment once made to me about my persistence. I had been introduced to Derek Coltman, the Director of Education at the Institute of Directors, as a person who could advise me on starting my scholarship for "The Most Promising Young Business Woman', which I now give annually. I had received initial reservations about it from Oxford, one of the universities I approached, based upon their fears that it could be discriminatory. 'I can't believe this can be true,' I told Derek. 'I have to find a solution.'

I consulted a friend of mine from Zonta a worldwide professional women's organization which I belong to, asking for ideas. She said, 'I know what to do. Margaret Thatcher is an honorary member of your London II club – we'll call Baroness Young who is responsible for education under Mrs Thatcher and ask her about it.'

The next day I called Derek to say I'd had a call from Baroness Young's office advising us that all was OK.

Some months later my husband and I had a party and we met Derek's wife for the first time. 'Ah, so you're Christine Harvey,' she said. 'I remember when Derek first met you. He said, "I know one reason that woman is a success – it's her persistence. When she gets an idea she doesn't give up, no matter what the odds are." '

Tom and I have known Derek and Basha for nine years now, but I'll never forget that first comment she made to me. It reinforced my own belief about persistence. Since then I've been able to draw upon it on numerous occasions when I needed to remember that, indeed, I did have the quality of persistence.

What incident in the past has given you proof that you do have the necessary persistence to get results? What goals do you have in your life *now* to which you could apply that persistence to get the results you want?

Think of someone you want to motivate, and about the effect Basha's comment had on me. Is there something you can say to show them that they do have the quality of persistence?

Sometimes people don't know their own strengths. In fact, *often* they don't know their own strengths. 'When you show them their strengths,' as I often say in my motivational speeches, 'they will follow you anywhere.' Showing people their strengths is a leadership quality. Who can you choose? What can you say?

2 Break your own targets into weekly segments

If you want dramatic results in improving your sales, and you only follow one piece of advice in this book, I suggest you follow this:

Breaking targets into weekly segments, and sticking to them, is the simplest most straightforward way of increasing your results.

I promise you that if you do it your results will be astronomical. I've seen it happen in all industries. It works. As Bill and I said in *Your Pursuit of Profit*, most management targets are too broad and ill-defined to get results. Targets have to be short term (weekly or less) so that salespeople can fix their own personal activity schedule to them. For detailed information on this subject read chapter 21 on Management Controls in that book.

Michael Camp takes it a step further and creates high, low, high, low target weeks each month. In his low target week he spends time arranging displays. Whatever industry you're in, there are always things to be done which 'there's never time for'. These can be essential to future sales. Why not try the high, low target system yourself, making time in the low week to tackle those essentials which are standing between you and the big-time results?

3 Get support for change by asking questions

'People only change when they want to change.' I said that in a sales management seminar in Singapore recently and one of the participants broke off her seven-year engagement with her fiancé as a result of hearing it. I was a little concerned, having heard about this later, as I didn't expect a management seminar to affect people's personal lives.

'Don't worry,' she told me later. 'It's the best thing that ever happened. I kept thinking I could affect change. When I realized that people don't change unless *they* want to, I saw things differently.'

For the rest of us, when we teach people to improve their performance in sales and in management, our job is not as difficult as in personal relationships. But the principles are the same. First, we need to inspire them to want to change. Camp does this by getting them to think the ideas are their own – by asking questions.

Whose performance do you want to change? Are you making the mistake our seminar participant made – are you thinking *you* can change *them*? Remember, to create changes they have to want to do it, and the best way you can support them is by asking questions. Why not review Michael Camp.s questioning process and try it tomorrow?

4 Four-part formula for turnaround success

Are you in a turnaround situation? It doesn't matter whether you're managing yourself or a team of people. The four principles Camp uses can bring you dramatic results.

Do you need to raise standards? Do you need to identify areas where you can build volume? Do you need to control costs? Do you need to raise morale?

Think through the list. Which one appeals to you most?

Go back over the way Camp approached each area and see how these procedures can be applied to your situation. How can you make a ten per cent shift in what you're doing now and get 100 per cent better results?

With regard to morale, if you're working on your own I have two suggestions. First, keep a small notebook and, at the end of the day, write down two things you did on the job that you enjoyed or got satisfaction from. Force yourself to do it no matter how hard or impossible it seems. After one week you'll have new spirit. Secondly, go back and reread the Action Section: 'Use a positive approach', Janet Lim (Chapter 2). Then let all thoughts which flow be positive. Start *today*, and tomorrow will be different.

5 Work closely with your distributors

The main message here is that Camp treated his distributors the same as his own employees. He gave them resources. He worked with them to develop strategies. He helped them identify the important customers. Then he applied the 80–20 rule and spent the most time developing the important ones.

In my own experience of working with companies, it always amazes me to see people appoint distributors and forget about them. Then they complain when they don't get results. I say to them, 'You wouldn't hire a rep and put them over in a foreign country and forget about them, would you?' No, of course not. They would send them with a briefing. They would communicate weekly. They would give them support. If they didn't get results, they would try a new strategy or a new rep.

It boils down to giving distributors the same support, or more, than you give your own people to get results.

What results do you want? What support do you give?

6 Influence all and develop a strategy

This is a big subject for a little space! There are volumes written on each of these two points. Yet Camp takes a common sense approach to it all and gets tremendous results. One of the things Bill Durning said about Camp which I didn't tell you in this chapter is that 'He has extraordinary common sense for a person of his years'. I agree.

Sometimes I think we try to be too technical about things. If we just stand back and use common sense, we go a long way.

Michael Camp looks for match between what he can offer and what the customer needs in order to sell more products. He thinks long and hard about it. Then, when he knows his strategy is right, he puts it down on paper so that it's easy to understand – he uses pie charts and graphs. *Voilà*, magic, they see it and they love it. But they're not sure others will love it. So Michael Camp talks to the others, too.

It's common sense. He's done them a favour. He's done his company a favour. Everybody profits.

What steps can you take to match what you have to what the customer needs so that everybody can profit? When you have the answer, talk to everyone about it.

We started this Action Section by saying, 'Use persistence when all else fails'. An equally valid point is, 'When all else fails – use common sense.'

I suppose that'a good way to end the book. You may not have a PhD in marketing or psychology, or a degree in anything for that matter which would put you in good company with many of the top performers of the world, but persistence and common sense will take you to amazing heights.

It's been a great pleasure to share these experiences with you and I hope you've enjoyed it too.

I hope it changes your life in some way, big or small. Write and let me know.

Yours sincerely,

Christine Harvey
Intrinsic Marketing
65 Blandford Street
London W1H 3AJ
England

Recognizing and Hiring High Flyers

Look at their early life activities. These are not usually requested on traditional job application forms.

At age 14 Janet Lim Lay Yang was working on a farm and on a construction site while going to school. Today she links much of her success to the ability to work hard.

At age five Ove Sjögren's grandfather was timing him for ski racing. At eight he was determined to win the ski championship and did.

At age ten Jonathan Weal had a team of four people washing cars. At 13 he was reading the *Financial Times*. At 14 he was skipping school to buy and sell antiques. These were all indicators of leadership, self-realization and determination.

Lack of experience in sales had little to do with Bob Broadley's success. Eight companies refused his services before he found one which agreed to give him a chance. Once in, he earned $20,000 in commission, then jumped to $92,000 with the next company.

Nor did lack of experience in sales stop Micheline Notteboom-Dusselier. By questioning her we see that she adopted her techniques of perfectionism, organization and working with people from a successful boss while working as his secretary.

Before becoming number one salesman at Electrolux, Ove Sjögren was a painter with no sales experience. He applied the same hard work ethics, determination and systems approach to sales as he had done to painting.

Honeywell's multi-million dollar salesman Denzil Plomer serviced autopilot systems during the war before starting his sales success. He applied his creativity to finding the best solutions for both jobs.

Michael Renz had technical training at college before becoming the Mercedes top sales performer.

Michael Camp was in the civil service and was impatient waiting for things to happen. In sales he makes things happen, breaking records for performance in every position he has held. He was turned down by four companies because he had 'no previous experience'.

Jon Bichener had never sold a thing before helping a friend turn a £20,000 debt into a £3.5 million company through telephone sales. He uses his fast style, efficiency and love of the work to achieve his high performance.

The lesson is loud and clear. It's the personal qualities of the person which makes them a success in sales, not their experience.

To recognize potential high performers, look for the extremes in personal qualities. Do they have more persistence, more perfection, more determination or more of anything which makes them unique and sets them apart from the others?

Recognizing high flyers requires creativity in the questioning process. It requires probing. It requires an open mind about capability versus experience.

That's assuming you can supply an environment which meets their needs.

Ask them: What do they want? Is it management support – is it competitive challenge – is it peer recognition – is it promotional possibilities – is it variety – is it responsive management – is it the opportunity to learn and to have self development – is it quality of product – is it the reputation of the company – is it adventure and travel – is it the opportunity to be creative? Each is different.

If you thought money was the one thing that mattered, think again. Money alone won't get them and won't keep them. Can you supply the environment which meets their needs?

Motivation and Managing High Performers

1: JONATHAN WEAL

'The most frustration I've felt was from management teams in which only ten per cent were doers. The other 90 per cent were people who either said "No", or "I'll think about it", or they'd delegate the decision. It usually never resurfaces or it gets completely lost in the legal department.'

Movers and shakers want support and they want it *now*. They identify what bottlenecks there are in the organization and they want them eliminated. They can't do their job without it. They won't settle for mediocrity.

It's all too easy for managers to say 'No' rather than support the high performers. As a result they lose their best people and their best marketing ideas. Granted, many suggestions may not work, but management needs to assess the cost of trying before rejecting them. Costs need to be measured in terms of: potential risk, potential gain, and morale of the high flyers they stand to lose. Managing high flyers means you have to make management decisions 'now'. High flyers won't wait! They'll move on.

2: JANET LIM LAY YANG

Janet moves fast. She doesn't want hold ups for herself or her customer. She puts notes on her boss's desk 'Good morning, Boss', asking for his assistance in getting paperwork and so on through.

She wants support to do her job faster and better. How is your support system for high performers?

3: BOB BROADLEY

Bob Broadley recognized a better way to sell. It was through free trial of machines. But management wouldn't listen. After he bought the equipment himself and raised the sales volume 24 fold in one month, they took notice and changed their policy.

If Bob hadn't had the conviction to prove his point, their sales volume would have remained low.

How often does management stick to its old way of doing things? What investment would it take to *try* new ways? For Bob's management, the financial investment would have been small.

4: MICHELINE NOTTEBOOM-DUSSELIER

Micheline uses persistence within the company to bring about good liaison between sales and production. Her management realizes that this co-operation is critical to success.

Other companies don't. They put barriers up between people and departments. Without co-operation they falter and die. What do you do to foster liaison between departments, especially between sales and service or sales and production?

5: MICHAEL RENZ

Michael was careful to choose a company which had the highest reputation for quality and professionalism. Because his own standards of operation and expectations for performance are high, he (and people like him) expect the same professionalism from whatever company they work for.

Without a highly professional company framework, people of these standards are like fish out of water. They'll seek greener pastures. What standards to your salespeople keep? Could this be a reflection of the company standards? If so, are the standards right or do they need changing?

6: JON BICHENER

Jon loves to increase his product knowledge through training. He loves the stimulation of training. He hates standing still. His management recognizes this. They have one of the highest investments in training per employee in the industry, as well as the highest profit per employee. Their investment pays off.

What's your company policy on training? Is it attracting high flyers? Is it developing people into high performers? Is it keeping them? Perhaps a bit of reflection on this will pay off.

7: THE SONY TEAM

'Our job descriptions are unclear. People take on more and more responsibility,' says Mitsuru Ohki of Sony Broadcast. 'People feel committed to make their projects a success because they created the idea,' says another manager. 'No one points a finger at you when you're wrong,' says another.

Niels Thomas, Principal Sales Engineer, sums it up when he says, 'People respect each other's place on earth. To make a team work, the people have to get along together. They have to use each other's expertise – it doesn't work in companies that have in-fighting.'

He's seen it *not* work in other companies. I've seen it and you've seen it, too. What type of company do you have? What can you do to make people better collaborators for the good of all – themselves, their customers and their colleagues?

8: OVE SJÖGREN

'It's not just the money that counts,' says Ove Sjögren. 'It's the satisfaction of "helping people".' He now has 12,000 customers who he feels are friends – people he has helped, people who tell their friends to buy from him.

That's a lot of recognition – 12,000 customers over a 16-year sales career. But Electrolux doesn't leave it to the salesperson to generate their own recognition. They do it, too. They have a highest sales in Sweden award, a highest sales in the world award (excluding the US branch, which is a separate company), a highest sales in a three-month period award, and so on. They understand the importance of recognition.

In my sales seminars I quote a survey done by Management Centre Europe showing that lack of recognition is one of the biggest stress creators in management.

In my experience working with people and companies around the world, I place the lack of understanding about recognition and lack of skill in recognition techniques near the top of the list of things that should be improved to increase results dramatically.

What score do you give yourself on your ability to give recognition?

9: DENZIL PLOMER

Plomer's management knew his strengths. They flew him half-way around the world to help secure a difficult order. They knew his strengths in dealing with people of other cultures and using his creativity and negotiating skills. Later, after he had helped win the order, he admitted that the odds were so stacked against them that they had given up the hope of winning. But Plomer used his skills and made it happen.

His people used him to the fullest. They pulled him off another project. They *knew* his strengths.

Sitting in your organization are people with strengths which go unrecognized. How do you need them? Where do you need them? Find their strengths and use them. They'll benefit. You'll benefit.

10: MICHAEL CAMP

Human beings run their lives according to their own patterns. Watch them, it's predictable. Michael Camp left the civil service for the private sector where he could be promoted on merit. Luckily his management recognized his skill and promoted him each time they saw an opportunity.

Often they created an opportunity. Many high performers like Camp want to keep pushing their skill and performance up one more notch. Others prefer a pattern of staying in one job, performing steadily without change. For those who want change, you'll lose them if you don't create opportunities for advancement.

Which they of high performers do you have? Look at their patterns. Do they require change often? What's the longest and shortest period they've gone without change? Now you know their preferred operating cycle. What can you do to provide an opportunity within that preferred cycle of change? Find it, supply it and you'll keep them.

Don't make the mistake of thinking they operate as you think they 'should'. They won't. They'll operate according to their own pattern.

Good luck and best wishes. Salespeople only stay at the top when they continue to improve their skills. It's the same in management.

Acknowledgments

The first person I want to acknowledge is you. They say in America that only five per cent of the population take time to read. In Europe the statistics are similar. Of these, the majority are readers of novels and general information material. That puts you in the elite minority of those who focus their attention on self-improvement material such as this.

Think of what life would be like without self development. Mr Morita, the founder of Sony Corporation was asked why he wanted to learn to fly a helicopter. He said that he likes to continue to learn new things in life to keep his confidence up.

It proves that you're in good company. If the Chairman of the Sony Corporation, a man who started the company in his own lifetime and brought it to the position it is today, feels the need to keep learning new skills, what about you and what about me? Surely self development is a major aspect of success and satisfaction in life. Surely our own self development has positive spin-off effects on others. Therefore you can acknowledge yourself as being part of the small fraction of the population who are educating themselves on self development.

Secondly, I want to acknowledge the management of the companies whose people I've included. Several expressed hopes that their contribution would raise standards. 'I hope these ideas will help your readers,' said Lars Werner, MD of Electrolux Sweden.

It's easy to think that all companies want the PR connected with being in a book, but it's not so. In a few countries the companies we approached feared being misquoted and didn't want their people interviewed. I can understand that, having been misquoted by the press myself on occasion. A few people feared that they would give away company policy or feared taking responsibility for the decision. But they were in the minority.

I can honestly say that every company included was genuinely enthusiastic about sharing their secrets of success with you. I gave them all the opportunity to review the material to be printed in the chapters, and yet they changed little or nothing after reviewing it. They were completely open about letting you into their worlds, which is an inspiring insight into the management of top performers.

Thirdly, I want to acknowledge Frances Kelly, whom I consider to be a great friend as well as an agent.

Before my first book, I used to think that meetings with agents and publishers sounded very glamorous! Now that I've been through it, I can tell you, it is. The feeling of collaboration, the exhilaration of bringing something new into the world is almost like childbirth. (It's also more exciting to get the news than to deliver the end product, but that's another story!)

To be a good agent, you have to have people skills to negotiate – with the writer and the publisher – and good analytical skills to deal with contract terms and infinite details. Frances has these and I admire her enormously for them. It's a rare individual who can do both exceptionally well.

To be a good publishing company, you have to have people with vision who are also good managers. Century Hutchinson has that. When I was invited to address their sales force about this book, their Chairman, Steven Warshaw, gave me one of the most original introductions I've had the pleasure of receiving anywhere in the world. He took the trouble to get the facts to prepare it. He took the time to be there to inspire the sales force and me, despite the heavy pressures which Chairmen face, thus showing his enthusiasm and support for the sales effort.

Their Editorial Director, Lucy Shankleman, and all their people have been as professional as they've been supportive and collaborative to work with, making my job a great delight. I thank them all.

If you've read this far, you're doing great. You may have noticed that acknowledgments are exactly what they say. They acknowledge the people who made the book possible.

And rightly so. If you want some more thoughts on how I feel about recognition see the Reflections section on 'Motivating and Managing High Performers'.

That brings us to the high performers themselves. To Jonathan, Janet, Bob, Micheline, Michael, Jon, Ove, Denzil and Michael and the Sony team – Mitsuru, Niels, John, Alan, Chris – I send a personal note. I feel as though I know you all as friends and I enjoyed every minute of working with you. I hope that what we've done together has led you to even greater self recognition. I wish you the very best, always.

And last, but not least, thanks goes to the family, friends and staff behind the scenes. I was fortunate to have three able and gifted research assistants from the AIESEC organization at different times during the writing of the book: Yasmin Yasseri from Germany, Alain Thys from Belgium and Margret Schmidt-Brueninghaus from Germany, each of whose contributions and dedications could fill pages. Yasmin kicked the project off with all the research which it entailed, Alain progressed with

contacts, finesse and imagination. Margret saw every detail through to
the delivery of the manuscript to the publisher. Their lives became
intertwined with the project and they will always have a special place in
my heart.

And for providing the balance which makes life truly rewarding, my
thanks go to my husband Tom for his unbeatable support, and to our
children Laurie, Darrin and Tommy for sharing the excitement of
discovery. Also, to my friends and collaborators in different corners of
the world who are working to make it a better place – the people at
BAWE, NAWBO, ZONTA, AIESEC, Young Enterprise, the Cham-
bers of Commerce, the management institutes of Britain, Australia and
Singapore, the IOD, the networks and the Enterprise Agencies and
Boards with which I'm associated – may the secrets of your own success
live forever.

TO TAKE YOUR SKILLS FURTHER

You may be interested in meeting Christine Harvey and working with her to develop your skills further. If so, there are three different programmes to choose from to meet your varying needs. These include a two-day intensive workshop on **'How to Succeed in Selling'** for salespeople of all levels who want to improve their performance dramatically, a two-day **'Develop Effective Sales'** seminar for managers who want to develop greater strengths in their programme, and a one-day seminar on **'Motivation and You – 3 Steps to Business and Personal Success'** for people who want to identify their personal strengths and reach high-level goals in business and personal life.

The various programmes are offered at certain times during the year at the British Institute of Management and the Institute of Directors, London, the Singapore Institute of Management and the Australian Institute of Management. They are also available 'in-house' for companies that want to improve their results and often incorporate a mix of salespeople, management and staff for the team-building of sales results.

For dates of public courses and costs of in-house programmes, post the response form to:

Christine Harvey
Intrinsic Marketing
65 Blandford Street
London W1H 3AJ

Indicate your interest below

☐ How to Succeed in Sales
☐ Develop Effective Sales
☐ Motivation and You – 3 Steps to Business and Personal Success
☐ In-house and/or ☐ public

Please indicate address to which you would like the information sent:

Name: _____

Full Address: _____

_____

(with Company name if relevant) _____

_____

Country _____ Post Code _____

FAX/TEL./Tx (optional) _____

_____

Index